D1007148

Gifts of
the Trellis

ML Pearson

USA

© 2010 by ML Pearson
All rights reserved.

ISBN1475177992
LCCN

Printed in the United States of America.

Preface

This is my story as best as I can tell it. The life expectancy of someone like me is roughly 49 years of age. I turned 48 this year. It is my desire to leave for my posterity a record of my life. More importantly, I want them to know why I believe. As I sat down and considered those events that have affected my life and relationship with God, I soon realized I have learned more from my trials than I have learned from my pleasures.

I have several hesitations in sharing this story. The first is that I believe in honoring my mother and father. But here again, I learned more from the dysfunctional aspects of my relationship with my mother than from our more harmonious interactions. Although I try in the text to bring attention to my mother's difficult circumstances, I would ask you, Dear Reader, to be sympathetic to her situation. In my mind, she is a hero for enduring all of her challenges. I debated whether or not to even include the problems with our relationship, but the fact that I did not have a fully functional parent impacted me deeply. (And this was no fault of either my mother or my father.) I'm not sure if the rest of my story makes sense without including those early years of my life.

The second reservation I have with sharing something so personal is that it is a spiritual journey. As such, I realize there are many who will not relate with spiritual experiences. If you, Dear Reader, consider matters of the heart and soul to be trite or unsophisticated, this book is not for you. I also recognize you may not share my religious beliefs, but I hope you will relate with the honesty of my feelings.

I suppose the only reason I am willing to lay my life before you is so I can be a witness that God does visit us in our afflictions. I promise you that if you will look for Him, He will make Himself known. This is my experience of how He did that for me.

Acknowledgments

I would like to thank my Butler 27th Ward Relief Society writer's groups for motivating me to complete these memoirs. Your comments and suggestions have been invaluable. I would also like to thank all those who read my memoirs and offered helpful and honest feedback. A special note of thanks to Dawn Thurston for giving generously of her time and talents in reviewing my manuscript. Her book, *Breathe Life into Your Life Story*, continues to be a tremendous resource for our groups. In addition to those I have mentioned here, it is my hope that the following pages will recognize all of those wonderful souls who have done so much to make my life sweeter and easier. And to you, Stephanie, for insisting I publish this work.

*This book is dedicated to the
spiritually wounded*

Contents

1

A HOLE IN THE WALL

I've seen God. Now, before you consider me some crazed, religious hallucinator, I say I've seen God in much the same way I also claim to have seen the wind. Think about it. Do you really see air, or do you see everything else through it? This is the story of how I stopped seeing *through* God.

My paternal grandmother wrote in her journal that when I was two, I told her, "My Heavenly Father loves me." I suppose this might not seem significant, except my mother and father were not religious. Both had rejected the faith of their Mormon families.

My earliest memories of religion came years later when I was in elementary school. I attended after-school Primary at the local Mormon Church, where the official name was displayed as The Church of Jesus Christ of Latter-day Saints. All that remains from those years is how much I disliked one of the girls my age. She told everyone I was going to marry Matthew, a boy in our class. Since boys were THE most disgusting thing on the planet at the time, I could hardly stand the shame.

One day after I turned eight, my father sat on the edge of his bed, buffing a pair of shoes with polish and a rag. When he noticed me watching, he set the shoe and rag aside and lifted me to his knee. With his head bowed, he took in a deep breath. He looked at me, his dark eyes apologizing, and his lips frowning for a moment before he began, "You know, now that you're eight, you can be baptized. Do you want to be baptized?"

I nodded, feeling myself tighten. Dad never talked about religion. It usually made him angry and turned his face sour as though he'd smelled something awful. But I did want to be baptized. All of my friends had already been baptized.

"Well, you know your Uncle Jack hasn't been able to have any kids of his own."

I studied my dad's face. With his dark hair combed back, every strand in perfect order, and his even features, I thought he was the most handsome man I'd ever seen. Even though he was talking about church stuff, his eyes weren't mad, they were soft and sorry. I nodded again and leaned in closer.

"Wouldn't it be nice if Uncle Jack could baptize you since he might never have the chance to baptize one of his own children?" He watched for my reaction, lifting his chin until his mouth formed a weak smile.

I thought about his question. When my friends had been baptized, their fathers helped them walk down the stairs into a font filled with water. Their fathers were the ones who gently lowered them under the water and lifted them up again. But I sensed my father wanted Uncle Jack to baptize me. I tucked my chin and looked up at him. "Uncle Jack can baptize me."

My dad let out a deep breath, smiled, and patted me on the back. I was too young to understand he wasn't prepared to perform the ordinance.

I vaguely remember sitting next to Uncle Jack, a younger and more slender version of my father, wearing my white dress, staring at the font filled with lukewarm water. I looked back to see my father and mother sitting behind me in the room with my older brother and sister, Rob and Sue, along with the other onlookers. Several of us were being baptized that day and the room was full.

The memory of wading through water with my dress clinging to my legs is lost, and I don't recall going under or holding my breath, but I will never forget the feeling in my body when it was done. For a brief moment, God held me. I knew it must be God because He hugged me from the inside out. I felt much the same when, after I had dried off and put on a clean Sunday dress, Uncle Jack laid his hands on my head in front of everyone and among other things said, "Receive the Holy Ghost."

Mom and Dad argued a lot. I knew their relationship hadn't always been difficult. Mom told me the first time she ever saw my father, she was a sorority girl at the University of Utah. At a dance, she noticed a sharply dressed, handsome fraternity boy messing around on the drums before the band started to play. She said to herself, *That's the man I'm going to marry.* By the time Mom married Dad, on May 25, 1957, Dad had graduated from law school, and Mom was writing for the society section of the *Salt Lake Tribune.* A photo of them, smiling at a Rotary Club function, was displayed on their bathroom counter.

One evening after my baptism, a high-pitched "crack" shot from their bedroom. I ran in to see blueberry syrup dripping from a hole in the wall above their bed. Dad had been so mad about something, he threw his bowl of ice cream into the wall. The hole remained there until after he died.

I don't remember much about when he left for his fishing trip to Mexico with a group of his friends, about a year after I was baptized. Whether he told me goodbye, or gave me a hug, I don't recall. But while he was gone, I had dreams. Every night I dreamt he died. With each dream, I woke myself up sobbing.

His thirty-ninth birthday was on June 10, 1971, four days after he was supposed to come home. Mom pulled me into her lap and held me there in the green rocking chair in our family room. "What should we get your dad for his birthday?"

I pushed away, looking into her face. Her jaw was more rounded than my father's, and she had a richer smile. Short dark hair framed her questioning eyes. *She didn't know? She didn't know he wasn't coming home?*

For the first time, I realized something of great importance had been communicated to me. I knew my father was not coming home, and I knew one day I would understand why. I did not recognize the irony of learning my Heavenly Father knew and cared about me by telling me I would be losing my own earthly father.

On the day of my father's return from Mexico, the phone rang. And I knew. After taking the call, Mom's large brown eyes flushed empty. She told me, "Go get your brother and sister."

"It's about Dad, isn't it?"

"Go get your brother and sister," she repeated, her eyes still vacant.

"He's not coming home is he?"

She winced. "Go get your brother and sister."

I don't remember how she explained there had been a mid-air collision involving the plane my dad was on and an army jet over the mountains in California. And I don't recall if there was emotion in her voice when she told us there had been no survivors except the pilot of the plane who had crashed into them. But I already knew.

Dad wasn't coming home.

That night we all slept in Mom's bed, below the hole in the wall now covered by a picture. Even my brother, Rob, who was almost thirteen, slept on the floor next to the bed.

In the middle of the night, Dad walked into the bedroom, carrying his suitcase. A jacket was draped over his arm. I sat up and stared at him as he put his things away in the closet.

"Dad? I'm so glad you're home. They told us you died in a plane crash."

He stepped out of the closet and looked at me. "I can't stay. Tell your mother I love her." And he left, walking back out through the open door.

The next morning, the vividness of Dad's return was still with me. I whispered to Sue, who was eleven, "Dad came home last night." The moment I said it, I regretted letting the words go. What if Sue made fun of me or accused me of lying?

"I know," she whispered back, "He kissed me on the cheek."

2

DRAGGING FEET

After my father died, it was my 11-year-old sister, Sue, who started going to church. Every Sunday she would get up early, take a shower, wash the short dark hair that made her look like a boy, and walk to the meetinghouse about a mile away by herself. She even put on a dress, something you normally couldn't pay her to do.

One night at dinner, Sue asked with some hesitation, "Mom, could we go to the temple as a family?"

When Mom looked up at her, Sue ducked her eyes. "If we could be sealed to dad, we could be a family forever."

Mom's hand dropped, the fork clinking against her plate. She looked at Rob and me before looking back at Sue, "We don't go to church, Susan. And you can't go to the temple unless you go to church." She stabbed a piece of chicken on her plate and continued eating as if the conversation was over.

But Sue didn't let it rest. It seemed every few days she asked Mom again, "Can our family please go to the temple?"

Before long, Mom made an appointment with the bishop, the leader of our local unit called a ward. The Church requirement was that we would need to wait a year after dad's death, and the whole family would need to get ready. Each of us would have to pay our tithing, live the Word of Wisdom, attend all our meetings, and meet with the bishop for his approval. It wasn't long before all of us were getting up early on Sunday mornings, showering, and going to church.

Some weeks Mom didn't go with us. Rob, Sue, and I would walk the mile to church together. Rob would have on nice pants with a collared shirt and tie, his short brown hair parted on the side still wet from the shower. His soft brown eyes and Sunday clothes made him look kinder than the Rob I knew who tried out all of his latest wrestling moves on me. Sue and I wore dresses with short socks and Sunday shoes. I think it made Sue happy when I told her, "Even in a dress, Sue, you don't look much like a girl." She was a tomboy. Not one of her dresses ever had a ruffle.

Mom missed some weeks because she didn't feel well. She hadn't felt well for some time. She had vague complaints of headaches and dizziness. A few months later, she was diagnosed with brain tumors. When Dr. Bruce Sorensen, a family friend, neighbor, and our bishop at the time, began the surgery at LDS Hospital to remove them, Mom's tumors were too vascular. She started bleeding profusely, and Dr. Sorensen didn't feel confident he could successfully finish. He terminated the surgery, sewed her up, and shipped her back to the Mayo Clinic in Rochester, Minnesota, where they might have better luck. Dr. Sorensen traveled with Mom and participated in the surgery completed there at the Mayo Clinic. I didn't know it then, but years later Dr. Sorensen confided he did not expect her to live.

Although she made it through the surgery and the trip back to Salt Lake, Mom had to relearn how to do everything from rolling over to standing. She had lost all sensation, leaving her body numb from the neck down. I think about this now and wonder what impact this must have had on her personality and emotions as well.

I still remember my mom's mother, "Nanny," sitting by Mom's bed in a loose dress covered with a flour-dusted apron, feeding spoonfuls of broth while Mom lay flat in bed. "Yes, just another spoonful now," Nanny would say, nodding her head with Mom's every swallow.

For an entire summer, Mom couldn't even sit up to eat. Sue and I alternated between staying with Nanny and Grandad, or Aunt Joyce and Uncle Lee—Mom's sister and husband who lived in Bountiful close to Nanny. Rob stayed with Munner and Grandpa Schoenhals, who were Dad's parents. They favored Rob since he was a boy; they didn't want Sue or me because we were girls and wouldn't be carrying on the Schoenhals' family name. Sue and I were grateful they took him. At least we could have some peace from Rob's teasing.

Mom did eventually walk again, but on a tilt. After we returned back home for the beginning of the school year, her shoulder left a mark down the length of our hall where she leaned for balance.

In preparation for going to the temple, we had to attend church. I confess I was embarrassed about Mom. As a result of her surgery, she walked as though she'd had too much to drink. I was only ten and worried what people at church might think since Mormons aren't supposed to drink. And I knew there were a lot of important people in our ward. Many of them were doctors, or prominent attorneys, or presidents of companies. At that time, we had the dean of the University of Utah medical school in our ward, as well as one of the justices of the Utah Supreme Court.

One Sunday after sacrament meeting, we waited for everyone to leave the chapel. We hoped to help Mom out of the building without anyone noticing how she walked. When members of the next ward started coming into the chapel, I looked at Sue. Her eyes opened wide with worry. From that look, I knew she shared my concerns. We stood in unison and literally pulled Mom out of the chapel, dragging her feet behind us.

When we got outside, Mom scolded us, "What are the two of you doing? For heaven's sake, let me stand up." She was furious as she held on to us for balance, working to get her feet underneath her until she could stand. I still feel terrible when I think about how we treated her.

You'd think I'd have realized the other members would be sympathetic, but I was young, and we were the "inactives" in the ward. The Relief Society didn't bring in meals, and I don't recall any visits from ward members offering help. It's possible they had offered and Mom had refused. She didn't like accepting help from anyone.

When we went to the Salt Lake Temple, we pushed Mom in a wheelchair. She needed to receive her own endowments first, and I'm sure the process of making personal covenants with God through a lengthy service was not easy for her. I remember being excited to go to the temple and be sealed to my family for eternity. I missed my dad. I saw him everywhere I went—holding some other little girl's hand, or catching a glimpse as he drove by in another car. I even saw him snowmobiling with another family.

I knew these men weren't really my dad. I just couldn't convince myself he no longer existed in a tangible form. The temple made sense of it all. We could be together forever—if he accepted the work done in his behalf.

My Uncle Jack stood in as a proxy for my father. I wore a little white dress full to the floor with long sleeves. Sue wore one just like it. Lucky for Sue, I don't think the dresses had any frills. Rob had on a white shirt, white tie, and white pants. Once again, he looked a lot nicer than the brother I knew who liked to stick tape on my arms so he could rip off the hair.

I wondered if I would see my dad in the Temple. I'd heard stories that some people could see angels from the other side. I walked into the sealing room with Rob and Sue. In the middle of the room, Mom knelt awkwardly at the altar across from Uncle Jack. I noticed her wheelchair tucked into the corner.

The picture is surreal to me now. The struggle for Mom's life was written in the hollows of her cheeks. The roundness in her face was gone, and her smile was not as wealthy as it had been before the surgeries. The back of her head was scarred and raw, barely covered with a new growth of hair. As she reached across the altar, her hands and arms moved haltingly, without coordination.

I could not see it then, but this was the reason my father had been taken. He was a social man, concerned about his standing and appearance. I would learn later he and my mother had attended a party where mom had tripped and fallen. On the way home, he scolded her for having too much to drink and embarrassing him in front of everyone. In all fairness, he didn't realize Mom had brain tumors, but remembering that picture of my mother at the altar, I now know we would have lost him anyway.

Several years ago, when I was 42, before my Uncle Lee died, he admitted to me that after my father left on that fateful fishing trip to Mexico, Mom told Uncle Lee she thought Dad would be filing for divorce when he returned home.

I did not see my dad in the temple that day when I was sealed to him. But once again, I felt God. For just a moment, as we knelt at the altar, he again held me from the inside out and whispered to my heart, "I know you. And you are mine."

Even if my earthly father didn't accept this work, and didn't want to be with me forever, I knew I belonged to someone.

3

ABSOLUTE NOTHINGNESS
ANSWERED

My father's death and my mother's illness left me feeling vulnerable. Experience had taught me, if anything could go wrong, plan on it. Fear took over my mind and distorted my personality as I went through a period of being terrified of everything.

If a car parked in front of our house, I worried someone was casing our home. I spied on the vehicle through our front-room window. "Mom, that car has been parked in front of the house for more than half an hour. Don't you think we should call the police?" After all, who was there to protect us? And as I saw it, we lived on the edge of civilization. There on the end of Vista View Drive, we were the last house before the hill dropped down into the Emigration Canyon, and behind us there was nothing but open fields and the Wasatch Mountains.

Mom sighed, having no energy to check on the object of my distress, "Go ahead and call the police if you're worried."

I knew the number (and back then it was not 911.) When the nice lady answered, I told her, "There's a car parked in front of our home and it's been there for more than half an hour."

The sweet lady on the other end asked, "Have you told your mommie or daddy? Maybe you should tell your parents."

"But I did," I answered, nervously twirling the phone cord on my finger, "and my mom told me to call you."

My behavior was often bizarre, such as pinning safety pins in my curtains. I figured if a burglar came into our home, he'd be like Monty Hall on *Let's Make a Deal*. "If you have safety pins in your curtains, I won't kill you." Or, "If you have an egg in your night stand drawer, I won't burglarize your room. I can't imagine why my psyche connected a popular show I liked at the time with my fears. It was totally irrational.

I also became obsessive-compulsive about checking the locks on our doors. If my mom had let me, I would have stacked furniture and books in front of every one of them. It didn't help that during this time, a female real estate agent was raped in the home for sale across the street. And to make it worse, neither Rob nor Sue seemed to notice our imminent danger.

Everywhere I went, I feared people were following me— truly alarming thoughts for an 11-year-old girl. Mom was too preoccupied to notice, and no one else seemed to appreciate my anxiety. I don't recall anyone ever asking, "Is something bothering you?" I recognized I was being irrational, and I could feel myself losing control. But what was I supposed to do if we had a fire or an earthquake? How would I get Mom out of the house? This required some thought since she wouldn't be able to navigate it on her own with the walker she now used. Once again, Rob and Sue didn't seem the least bit anxious about this problem.

Each day as the sun set, the ensuing darkness magnified my fears. Every night became an internal struggle for sanity. I finally turned to prayer. I did so reluctantly since God seemed too far away to be of much help if someone burst through my doorway. I can't even say I prayed. It was more like begging—a silent, desperate plea for help. And yet, as time passed, prayer healed me.

I cannot claim any great revelations or miraculous events, but for those brief moments at night when I cried out in my mind, I was the one directing my thoughts with hope, instead of fear directing them for me. With each night's passing, I turned aside that feeling of terror and looked beyond my ceiling, placing my life in God's hands, trusting that if I didn't listen for intruders, I would still be alive the next morning.

Enter adolescence. I was devastated to enter puberty. When I turned twelve, I opened the big present Mom had bought for me. Thankfully, she gave it to me in the privacy of her bedroom, away from everyone else and separate from my other family gifts. Full of excitement, I removed the bow and peeled back the bright paper. I opened the box and turned back the tissue paper to discover a bra.

I couldn't look at my mother, and I never thanked her for the gift. I hid it under my bed and cried. I didn't want change. Change meant loss and I'd had enough of that already. If it hadn't been for Mom's bringing to my attention the obvious need for her gift, I probably wouldn't have worn it, either.

During this time, Mom was still trying to recover her own life.

We came home from shopping one day. Mom was driving, I was sitting in the back, and Sue was in the passenger seat. As we pulled in to our sloped driveway, the car continued forward. Mom looked down as we headed straight for the garage. She showed no signs of stopping the car. I braced for impact as we hit the bricks alongside the garage door.

Mom stared at Sue and me, wide-eyed and confused. "I couldn't find the brake pedal."

After all, her feet were numb. She never drove after that. This is why I started driving, without a license, when I was only fourteen.

Mom had also lost the ability to cook or clean, pay bills, or do laundry, but she could still supervise. And being the youngest, I was the easiest target. Luckily, she hired a woman to cook and do light housekeeping. Veda was an older, grandmotherly looking woman who was a polygamist wife from Eugene, Oregon. (I might also add that she was NOT Mormon. Mormons officially discontinued the practice of polygamy in 1890.) As fascinating as her story might have been, she treated herself as though she were a servant. She would never converse or show any hint of personal preference. While Veda took care of cleaning the house, cooking, and doing laundry, Sue and I took care of Mom.

Since Mom couldn't take me shopping, some of mother's good friends brought over clothes for me to wear. Though grateful for their kindness and all they gave me, when I started junior high at Clayton Middle School, none of my clothes were in style and most didn't fit. This certainly didn't build my confidence.

I stand by my belief that junior high is the armpit of life. Everyone at that age has an insatiable need to be popular. It doesn't take long before everyone has you pegged on the social ladder. And I knew right where I belonged.

When I started junior high, I had long hair I curled every day. I found everyone fun and friendly. I had no idea what the word "clique" meant. After about a month, I had a perm that ruined my hair. Uncle Lee, who was a barber, cut it all off. No one would speak to me after that. At first I didn't understand what was happening. I stood by a girl who had been a friend and asked her by name, "Why won't you talk to me?"

She never did answer. No one else would, either. I wasn't cute anymore.

It's tragic we go through these experiences when we're so immature. The way I saw it, if nobody else liked me, how could I possibly like myself? I was miserable. I hated myself and the family I belonged to. I became self-absorbed and thoughtless.

One day, Mom called to me from upstairs, "Could you come get me something to eat?"

I knew she couldn't get it for herself, but I was downstairs and I was watching television. I answered with disgust, "Didn't you eat yesterday?"

I wince every time I think about that. But there they are, those mean, ugly words I actually said to my own mother. Those words haunted me. As I grew older, and much of Mom's care fell to me, I considered it due punishment for how I had treated her on that one occasion.

Add to this, I was still terrified at night. At the end of every awful day I was so full of despair, I prayed God would take me. He was the only one I could talk to, and every night I pleaded my case. My life was so worthless; couldn't He just take me back home?

One day at school, in the middle of a busy hall, a boy pulled open the cowboy shirt I wore. I was mortified because I was sure everyone had heard about it and was making fun of me. That night I poured out my soul once again. I sobbed and confessed everything, noting my every mistake and every weakness and admitting to myself and to Him my absolute nothingness. I knew I had no right to ask Him for anything and certainly had no business expecting anything anyway; but I wanted Him to know I loved Him and appreciated His being my only friend.

That night, He answered. I felt Him wrap His arms around me and heard Him whisper to my mind, "I understand." He filled all the empty spaces in my heart and stayed with me the whole night, so I wasn't afraid. I would come to cherish this feeling as I had more of these experiences throughout my life.

Although Mom was limited in her mobility, she still enjoyed traveling. She spent her days planning road trips for us to take. The year before, the four of us—Rob, Sue, Mom, and I—took a trip to San Francisco. Rob drove and we transported Mom everywhere in her wheelchair. She was still in charge, telling us where to go and what we had to see. During adventures such as cable car rides, we just parked her somewhere and met back up with her when we were done.

Luckily, Rob had actually grown up into a nice, kind brother by this time.

One event that would have a huge impact on me later in my life occurred when I was in my last year of junior high. Before school was out, Mom had signed us up to go on a tour with the Utah Symphony back east to Washington, D.C. and New York City, as well as the British Isles, visiting England, Wales, and Scotland.

I didn't want to go. I had a mad crush on a boy who didn't know I existed, and I couldn't bear the thought of not being able to see him. I didn't know if he would go to my same high school. Since I couldn't admit this, I had no excuse, and Mom insisted I go with the family. This trip also included Aunt Joyce, Uncle Lee, and their three children, along with Nanny and Granddad, and a close widowed family friend we called Aunt Ruby.

While in Washington, D.C., the twelve of us took a tour of the Capitol Building. I kept noticing young people dressed in dark suits.

"Who are those kids?" I asked our tour guide.

"Those are pages," she answered. "They are high school students working for members of Congress."

"Oh." I didn't think about it again. At least not then.

4

LEARNING TO APPRECIATE

After discovering what it felt like to be encircled in the arms of His love, I looked forward to talking with God every night. I would tell Him all about my day, honestly evaluating myself and admitting my shortcomings. At one point, I was particularly disappointed in myself that I had no talents. Other kids benefited from lessons and natural abilities, of which I had none. This bothered me for several weeks until God whispered that maybe I should make it my talent to appreciate everyone else's.

This was encouraging. This was something I could do.

One girl in my history class gave a remarkable presentation. Where the rest of us were self-conscious and monotone, she had confidence, smiled, and spoke with animation. When class was over, I cautiously approached her. She was, after all, a lot more popular than I was.

I swallowed hard and could hardly look at her, "You, um, did a really good job. Um, I liked your, um, presentation."

She stared at me as though she had never seen me before and I was some weird-legged-thing that had crawled out from under an old log. Without responding to my compliment, she picked up her books and made a quick departure.

I wilted.

That night I talked with God about my challenge. I thought developing this talent would be easy. Instead, I felt even more inadequate. He whispered back, "Don't worry about what people think of you; focus on how you feel about them."

What a difference this small suggestion made. When another girl performed a skit for a school assembly, and it was hilarious, I found her in the hall. I looked her in the eye and said, "You were amazing."

She looked at me sideways as though she had never seen me before and wondered who I was to speak to her?

I just smiled back and walked away repeating over and over to myself, "I like her, I like her, I like her." It really didn't matter anymore what anyone else thought of me.

What a release. I had not perceived the power other people's opinions had over me. I lived through their perceptions where I had no control. I had allowed them to determine how I felt and what I thought. Now I was entitled to my own opinion. I was free. If they had a talent, I needed them to know I appreciated it.

I even told people I didn't like that I appreciated their talent. One girl I lockered next to, who generally ignored me, tried out for cheerleader. What could I do? She was a really good tumbler.

I swallowed hard and almost whispered, "You did a great job in the tryouts today. You are a really good tumbler."

This is the funny part; after saying that, it changed my opinion of her. I couldn't not like her anymore. It was the same with everyone. The more I told people the good I noticed in them, the more I liked them. That didn't necessarily mean they liked me, but that didn't matter.

I noticed another benefit. Before, when kids did amazing things, it made me feel small and less significant. I secretly wanted them to fail so they'd know how miserable I felt. But now, when they did something great, I felt bigger. I appreciated them more. By acknowledging their accomplishments, I felt more talented as well.

I admit there were times when the person was too intimidating, or so vastly beyond my social sphere, I could only imagine in my mind what I would have said to them if I'd had more confidence. Even though I couldn't tell them directly, it still changed the way I felt about them for the better.

I look back now and see the majesty and simplicity of God's hand. He framed my understanding of success as being connected to the success of others. It forced me to focus on everything good. And it completely reoriented my personality, my attitude, and how I saw myself in relation to others. As a terrified, self-loathing adolescent, I never would have thought to discover myself in the talents of others.

As I entered high school, I was acutely aware of how many skills I lacked. People knew I appreciated their abilities, but beyond that, I had no social skills. I constantly said stupid things, and when it came to boys, I was useless. I couldn't talk to a boy, especially if he was one I liked. Sue wasn't much help. By this time, we had drifted into our own adolescent orbits.

Once again, I became discouraged by how much I had to overcome. About this time, I went with Rob to receive our patriarchal blessings. These are blessings given by a Church patriarch that provide guidance and direction for one's life. In addition to being symbolic of the blessings given by the ancient patriarchs in the Old Testament, such a blessing generally identifies special strengths the individual has, promises specific things that can be achieved, or offers specific warnings. I was fifteen and Rob was preparing to go on his two-year Church mission to preach the gospel of Jesus Christ.

For several days before we went to receive our blessings, I worried the patriarch would place his hands on my head and have nothing to say. Fortunately, he relayed important messages. He gave me hope and direction that I would come to know what I needed to accomplish during my life. I received guidance regarding the person I was to marry and suggestions to keep in mind when raising my children. The scope of my blessing spanned from my lineage in the House of Israel through Ephraim, to the eternal sphere after my death. Best of all, it assured me that God knew me. He knew me better than I knew myself. He saw me as one with unlimited potential, which at that time, I could not see. Over the course of my life, He promised to reveal me to myself.

This blessing has been a source of comfort and clarity. As I've aged and matured and experienced life on different levels, the words and phrases have taken on new meaning and provided beautiful insight into my divine purpose. But as an inexperienced and nervous teenager, it provided the immediate blessing of allowing me to look forward to the future.

God became my parent. Every night, I was honest with Him. I admitted all of my mistakes, figuring He knew about them already, but what a relief to let them go. I never felt any condemnation, just a whispered assurance that every day was a new opportunity for improvement. Knowing I was probably blind to my most obvious flaws, I sought His advice on overcoming my weaknesses.

One big area I needed to work on was loving my mother and being more willing to serve her. So many times she expected me to fulfill her responsibilities and I was often resentful. For example, at Sunday dinners out at Nanny's with all the cousins she'd look at me and say, "Go out and do the dishes." There she was, confined to the recliner where Uncle Lee had placed her after lifting her from our car. Not only had I fixed her plate, and fed her, but now she insisted I go out and do the dishes.

I was fifteen. The only people who did dishes were my aunts and Nanny. I didn't know how to step in as a grandchild and tell my "elders," "Move aside. I'm here to do dishes." I resented that more was demanded from me than from any of my other cousins who were, for the most part, older.

Mom would say with exasperation, "Can't you see what needs to be done?"

I tell you honestly, I couldn't. Maybe that was a deficit that came from never seeing a mother in action. I had never seen her set or clear a table. I could not remember her doing dishes. How was I supposed to know how to do these things? I admit I didn't do the dishes, but I did learn how to clean off the several large dining room tables Nanny used to feed her clan. (She fed 30 to 40 of us every week.)

About this time, Rob left on his mission to Munich, Germany. Sue graduated from high school and went away to college at Utah State University in Logan, Utah.

With the two of them gone, I would wake up, get ready for school, and hang Mom's clothes for the day on her walker. I'd fix her Pero, a warm drink made from roasted grains, and toast, leaving them on the kitchen table for breakfast. I would make her lunch and stick it in a sack in the refridgerator. When I came home from school, I was responsible for paying the bills, running errands, and grocery shopping, along with all of my homework and high school activities.

"The toilet downstairs isn't flushing," I told Mom one day. Every time I pushed the lever for it to flush, nothing happened. The handle just dropped and came back up with no resistance.

"Well, since no one will see it, we just won't use that one then," Mom answered.

That's how it was. Mom did not have the energy and I didn't have the time to complicate things, especially if it was something I couldn't take care of and something Mom didn't have to look at. When water leaked through the downstairs foundation, I simply pulled back the carpet until it dried. In the middle of winter, our sliding door came off the track. If I could have locked that door, which led to our back patio, and if a small drift of snow hadn't collected on the carpet from a blizzard where Mom could see it, we probably would have left it. I don't know how many days it was before Mom called a neighbor to help. She hated bothering other people with our problems. If anything broke, unless it was something we absolutely needed, we just didn't use it anymore.

With regard to my mother, as I prayed, I felt impressed that when I did anything for Mom, I should do it because I *wanted* to not because I *had* to.

I pulled into the driveway from school, knowing Mom had her to-do list ready. Since she couldn't write things down, I knew she had repeated her list over and over during the day so she wouldn't forget anything.

I opened the back sliding door ready for the onslaught.

Mom was sitting at the kitchen table, leaning forward, ready to begin, "It's my friend, Jean's, birthday today so I need you to go to Jensen's Floral and buy her some flowers. Call them right now and tell them you want a bouquet of flowers that includes white daisies, but you want an assortment."

I dropped my backpack to the floor by the door and struggled against the resentment that washed over me by reminding myself: *She needs you; she can't do this for herself; you want to do this for her.*

"Did I tell you her daughter was just accepted to Wellesley, that prestigious all-girl Ivy League college? I must say, Jean has the most impressive children."

Mom paused. She shook her head and wriggled her nose, trying to dislodge something from her face. When that didn't work, she extended her lower lip so she could puff her breath up to blow it away. When that still didn't work, she lifted her arm. It moved awkwardly and since her fingers were incapable of individual movement, she used the palm of her hand and ended up hitting herself in the eye instead.

I moved closer until I could see the offending stray hair that had fallen over her eye and across her cheek. I pulled it away, allowing it to drop before taking my position at the other end of the table.

Mom continued, "Put my name on the card and take them by her home. I also need you to write a check out to Aunt Joyce for my theater ticket for $60 and send it to her."

I want to do this for her. I want to do this for her. I repeated this over and over until it felt true and I had convinced myself.

For a time, the burden of caring for Mom and being her arms and hands affected me deeply. I wondered if caring for her was like having children. If so, I didn't want kids. For several weeks this feeling festered. I became obsessed with not wanting children. Then I had a dream. A little blonde-haired boy kept reaching out for me. Instead of resenting his need for me, his need filled me. He was mine and I loved him without effort. When I awoke, I felt so relieved to know there was a difference and that I would enjoy being a mother. I had no idea at that time how much faith and sacrifice would be required to actually obtain that little blonde-haired boy.

But there were times when I struggled with meeting Mom's needs. On a few occasions, I tried talking to her.

One night after a difficult day, I helped Mom change into her nightshirt. She sat on the side of her bed as I hung up the shirt and pants she had worn that day in her closet. I still had to write an essay due the next morning as well as a finish a project for my history class. Mom waited for me to help lift her legs up on the bed. "Don't forget to make out Veda's paycheck and then you need to fill out and send in the tax form for household employees. Tomorrow you also need to go through the closets and take what we don't need to the Junior League. They're having their open house next week."

I added those things to my list, wondering how I could get it all done, especially when Mom didn't seem the least bit concerned about my life and assignments due.

"I've also noticed the back porch is covered in debris that's blown down from the field. You need to get that cleaned off." She pulled at the upright pillow with her hand, using the small space between her thumb and palm to grab the corner of the pillow and lay it flat on the bed.

I walked out of the closet, breathing heavy with frustration. "Mom, I have a lot of school work due this week."

"You do realize that porch is the first thing people see when they come to the door?"

Could she not hear me? "Mom, sometimes I feel like I'm drowning underneath all of your expectations. I can't even finish one thing before you've given me ten more to do."

"It would be so much easier," Mom said, shutting her eyes and shaking her head, "if you wouldn't wait for me to tell you what to do and you could just do it without having to be told. Can't you see what needs to be done? That debris has been on the porch for weeks. I shouldn't have to ask you to do everything."

I waited for Mom to lean over on her pillow before I lifted her legs up on the bed. "But you don't even give me the chance." I winced. "I actually do have school and homework and other responsibilities on top of everything you demand."

Her face grew quiet, the still before the storm, as she rolled over on her back. She waited until I had pulled the covers up and tucked them in around her before saying, "Do you have any idea how selfish and ungrateful you are?"

I soon realized that not only could Mom not hear me, she could not see me either. She was blinded by her inability to meet her own basic needs, her being shut-in, and her dependence on me for almost everything. Not to mention the brain trauma from her surgeries that affected her in countless, unseen ways. She simply was unable to view the world from my perspective and recognize the overwhelming weight I shouldered.

I ended up sharing my burden with God instead.

Truthfully, the burden didn't change. If anything, it became more difficult. Mom was losing function and complaining of "feeling pressure." Doctors discovered an extensive cyst running the length of her spinal cord. She needed surgery to place a shunt in her cord to reduce the fluid, and hopefully, the pressure.

While Mom was in the hospital, Aunt Joyce and Aunt Lois, two of her sisters, pulled me aside and chastised me for not taking better care of my mother. With short red hair and glasses hanging around her neck, Aunt Joyce folded her arms. Among other things she said, "You should be taking your mother for rides in the car so she can get out of that house."

Aunt Lois nodded. Her hair was equally short, but dark and speckled with gray. "You need to bring her out to Bountiful more often."

I knew that in Mom's frustration, she vented to Aunt Joyce everyday on the phone about what wasn't getting done. There were times when I couldn't help but overhear Mom's end of the conversation. And I knew the exhaustive list of her complaints.

But I was devastated and confused. Aunt Joyce and Aunt Lois were upset with me for not doing more, when they rarely came to help meet Mom's needs. Their comment was always, "Well, if you lived closer, we could help." They lived in Bountiful, about fifteen miles away. And in fairness, perhaps they had offered to help, but Mom had refused.

Regardless, they couldn't see me either. And how could they? They had never been in my position. They wanted me to mother my mother, when I had never had a mother who could show me how.

Even though the burden of taking care of Mom didn't change, God changed me. He opened my mind and heart to the reality of human nature without judgment. Just as Aunt Joyce and Aunt Lois could not understand my situation, I could not understand theirs. I knew they had chastised me out of their concern and love for my mother. I had no right to judge them, but I needed to be very careful in my own life not to expect something from someone else that I was unwilling to do myself. I knew how that felt.

The same went for my mother. Perhaps I was ungrateful, but given how much I did for her everyday, she never said, "thank you," or showed any sign of appreciation for what I did to help.

This was the reality of human nature I came to accept. As I matured through experiences of my own later in life, I came to a deeper understanding of my mother's situation—the losses she had suffered, the limitations she endured, and the burdens she shouldered. As a teenager, I could not fully appreciate what it meant to be a widow rearing three children while facing a life-threatening illness that plundered her body's function.

But God knew. I'm sure that's why He encouraged me every time Mom asked me to do something, to make sure I sincerely wanted and enjoyed doing it for her.

I also promised myself that if anyone did anything for me, even the smallest act, I would show my appreciation and be grateful. This was, perhaps, one of the most important lessons of my life.

5

POSITIVE FEEDBACK

Positive changes began to take place. I attribute this to God's hand and guidance in my life. Quite a statement I realize, but knowing my own personality and my difficult circumstances at home, I wouldn't have had the strength to pull myself through on my own. I developed a new confidence. God loved me. No matter what else happened in my day, I could talk it over with Him and be assured He cared. If I had a problem, I knew He would help me.

I attended East High School and I was a 4.0 student. (I am now rubbing my knuckles on my shirt.) I had a place on the debate team led by a charismatic and popular teacher. By this time, I had developed a close group of six girlfriends. We associated with some of the cutest boys in the school, who were also on the debate team. I'll never forget the day when one of the most popular girls in my grade said, "Hello," to me. (Maybe my hair had grown longer.) I auditioned for Pep Club, a prestigious marching and cheering squad, and not only made it but was elected as an officer. (Blowing on my knuckles.)

On one occasion, I received a compliment. Perhaps my English teacher told me my essay on Shakespeare was the best she had read that year. Whatever it was, to me it was big and I remember being so happy. I came home and told Mom, expecting her to be happy too, and in some way be proud of me. I knew how much honor, prestige, and academic achievement meant to her.

Mom looked at me without smiling. "Are you the best in every subject?"

My smile faded as I considered her question. I shook my head. "No."

She nodded her approval. "You need to remember that. No matter how good you are, there will always be someone better."

I bit my lip and backed away.

She was certainly in a difficult circumstance, but I don't recall receiving *any* positive feedback. Not ever. She never once told me she loved me or gave any physical affection. I desperately wanted to know she valued me, and my desire for excellence was an effort to make her proud. I knew how important accomplishment was to her, but no matter what I achieved, it never seemed to please her. Whenever I told her about something good that happened to me, her response was the same—"No matter how good you think you are, there will always be someone better."

I talked to my Father in Heaven about this and how discouraged I was. He whispered back that He cared and He wanted to know about all the good things that happened to me. I was also prompted to write them in my journal where I could remember them. That way, when I was discouraged, I could look back and gain strength from all the good in my life.

He also taught me about humility. And Mom's response was essentially the world's reaction. People would not be interested in my success. Human nature again. I came to terms with the reality that God was the only One who needed to know.

From that time forward, I stopped telling Mom about any of my successes. I didn't tell her when I made Dance Company (and I had never had the benefit of dance lessons) or if I won a debate. Knowing that Rob would be home from his mission the summer before my senior year, and Sue would be home from her study abroad to England (which she did after one year at Utah State), I didn't even tell Mom when I applied to be a Page in Washington, D.C., for my senior year.

I don't know why I applied. At that particular time in my life, the thought of those young people walking through the halls of the Capitol Building kept coming back into my mind. I'd seen them several years earlier on our trip with the Utah Symphony, and hadn't given it much conscious thought since.

As I shared my joys with God, He encouraged me to love and accept my mother. On a difficult night when I was struggling with Mom's demands and lack of nurture, He challenged me to tell her I loved her. This did not come from me. If on some occasions I wondered if every night I was just talking to myself, this was proof I wasn't. The idea of telling my mom I loved her would NEVER have occurred to me. Not once in my life had I ever heard anyone say to me, "I love you."

I shrank, alone in my bed. I mouthed the words, "I love you," and they seemed awkward and foreign. I couldn't imagine saying them to my mom, but I trusted God. Sometime later, while Mom sat at the kitchen table, watching our 13-inch, black-and-white television, I stood by her and said, "Mom?"

She turned with her shoulders to look at me, waiting for my question.

I bent down, reached my arms around her stiff body, gave her a tentative hug, and said, "I love you."

Forgive me for not remembering what happened. As I recall, she remained stiff, not making any attempt of a physical or verbal response. I don't recall any acknowledgment or emotion.

After writing those words, I had to call my sister. "Was Mom really that cold?"

"Yes," she answered. "But remember, Mom was never told she was loved either. It was a generational thing." Sue went on to say that later in her life, she had been listening with Mom to a tape by Garrison Keeler about *Lake Wobegon*. The story was of a baseball coach who loved his team but never gave his kids any praise. They were the best in the county, but he never acknowledged how good they were, afraid if he did, the kids would stop trying to be better. Mom looked at Sue and said, "That's how I've raised you."

I have never met anyone who had a perfect childhood. For every one of us there are puncuation marks in our past that make us pause. These question marks and exclamation points can take different forms such as tragic events, or destructive relationships, but all of us have suffered some form of anguish during our vulnerable childhood years.

A few years ago, I was helping my son review for a physics test. He had to memorize the amount of heat energy it took for one gram of ice to melt into water, boil, and then turn into steam. Each one of those changes to a higher level, that seemed to happen so naturally and effortlessly, took an enormous amount of energy. This realization led me to ponder. Change for the better in each one of our lives must also require additional power and a need to draw from a source of energy.

By encouraging me to tell my mother I loved her, when I was still a child and had never been told I was loved, God blessed my past. By responding to my pleas for help during those challenging times and allowing me to experience these events with an understanding heart, God blessed my life. He was the power fueling each positive change in my childhood.

I see things from a wider perspective now, my mom without a spouse, unable to meet her own needs, relying on a selfish teenager to take care of her. How discouraged she must have been. I think back to that day when I so awkwardly put my arms around her, and I'm not certain, after all she had been married, but I wonder if I was also one of the first to tell her she was loved.

6

ANGELS AMONG US

Michele met me at the Washington, D.C., airport. Michele was my neighbor and good friend back in Salt Lake City. She was taller, skinnier, and smarter than I. We lived on Vista View Drive, and she lived on Millicent, two streets over and one house away from Aunt Dixie and Uncle Jack, my father's only brother. When I applied to be a page for the House, Michele applied to be one for the Senate. Our tenures would be different. Michele would be a page for two months, and she'd already been in Washington, D.C., for one of those, but I would be there for my entire senior year. Knowing that Mom had Rob back from his mission and Sue from her study abroad, I figured she'd be in good hands until I returned.

I arrived in Washington, D.C., on Labor Day, September 3, 1979, and lucky for me, Michele already knew the ropes. I had to pinch myself as Michele and I jumped on the Metro at the airport. I had applied to be a page at the beginning of my junior year and hadn't heard anything for months. When I finally worked up the nerve to call the office of Dan Marriott, my congressman at the time, I was told my application had been lost, but it didn't really matter because the congressman could only sponsor one applicant, and his Administrative Assistant's daughter had already applied. But in February, I received a letter informing me that my application had been forwarded on to the committee and wishing me luck because "The competition for these positions is very keen since we Republicans have only twelve of the seventy-two page appointments."

At the completion of my page experience, Barry Nielsen, Dan Marriott's Administrative Assistant wrote me this note, "I remember clearly your letter to us requesting appointment as a page in the House. I also remember our initial inquiry into it and finding the odds against your appointment were very great because of Dan being a Republican and of low seniority. As I recall, we were told there was no chance. Things changed. It was obviously your destiny to be assigned."

I certainly felt this on my first Metro ride to our dormitory, Thompson-Markward Hall, which was located within a block of the Supreme Court Building and on the same side of the street as the Library of Congress, my new school.

After settling into my new room at the Hall, just a small space with room enough for a bed and desk, Michele and I started our way down the road to Pennsylvania Avenue where we could get some food. Cat-sized animals criss-crossed the sidewalk in front of us. I kept looking at them scurry, trying to figure out what they were. I had never seen anything like them before. They had whiskered snouts, and a long thin tail. When I realized they were rats, I shuddered. How did they ever get so big? And why were there so many of them?

We walked past the Supreme Court Building and I had to stop, replant my feet, and orient myself. I had seen pictures of this building, but with no appreciation of its enormity or the gigantic scale of the human figures flanking the stairs. Each statue alone weighed 45 tons and the "little" statue of Justice the woman held in her hand was itself 4.5 feet tall! For the entire time I served in Washington, I was constantly in awe of the architectural scale of every building, statue, and monument. I am still left with a sense of magnificence.

ANGELS AMONG US

As Michele and I continued our walk to Pennsylvania Avenue, I noticed a man walking towards us. He looked filthy, and the closer he came, the dirtier he seemed until we were just ready to pass him. His shirt wasn't dirty, it was bloody, and his bruised face wasn't filthy, it was crusted with drying blood. "Watch your step, girls, watch your step."

I looked around and the street seemed eerily abandoned with the exception of the darting rats. Michele explained, "It's empty because it's a holiday, this place is busy during the week days." But it wasn't lost on me that this was not a safe city and the stranger had given me some sage advice.

Safety would be a major issue for me during my stay in Washington. I learned that over and over again, but I also realized I was being watched over. Before Michele's final month was up, we heard that President Spencer W. Kimball, the President of The Church of Jesus Christ of Latter-day Saints, was coming to speak at an arena outside of the D.C. limits. I believed he was God's prophet, and I wanted to hear him. This was my idea: we would catch a bus and ride it to the end of its route, where we would take a taxi the rest of the way. After the service, we would find a ride with someone to the place where we would catch the bus again. Things did not go exactly as I had planned.

On September 9th, the Sunday after my arrival, Michele and I boarded a bus to take us to the arena. We rode it to the end of the line and got off. We stood on a traffic island, waiting for a cab. We were in the middle of a ghetto. Iron bars covered the shop windows, some of which had been broken anyway. Debris and graffiti littered the streets. Michele and I had not stood there for more than twenty seconds when a car pulled up beside the island and an African-American woman got out. She didn't say a word, but stood right there by our side.

Michele and I looked at each other thinking this was a bit strange. About twenty to thirty minutes later, a cab came and picked us up. We didn't think anything of it. We attended the conference and heard President Kimball speak.

President Kimball was born in 1895, had been ordained an apostle of Jesus Christ in 1943, and became the Prophet and President of the Church in 1973. He was now 84 years old. Having suffered from throat cancer, he spoke with a raspy and tender voice. I was touched as he spoke of his being accountable to God for his life, his words, and his actions. It impressed on me that I was also accountable to God for my life and all my choices. He concluded his remarks by bearing witness of the Father and His Son, for whom the Church he represented was named.

As we sang the closing hymn, I panicked realizing we needed a ride back to the ghetto stop where we could catch the bus. I looked around me. All of these people were Mormons. One of them would be happy to give us a ride, wouldn't they?

Since Michele was even more shy than I, and this whole thing had been my idea, I took the lead in asking people for a ride. I started by asking people in the arena. If I had been in Salt Lake, people would not only have been happy to give us a ride, they would have been interested in where we were from and what we were doing being so young and living away from home. But there in D.C., no one would even speak to us. I would ask, and they would completely ignore me.

We made our way out into the parking lot, filled to capacity with station wagons. I would go up to a car and ask if there was any way we could get a ride and all the doors would shut, locks would engage, and windows would roll up. It wasn't as if we looked scary. We were in our Sunday dresses, carrying our scripture cases. We were both sixteen, straight out of Salt Lake City, and even had Utah accents. I remember sitting on the curb in front of the arena, the security people and cleaning crew one-by-one filing to their cars, and leaving the lot empty.

I'm not an emotional person, but my eyes welled up, and it was all I could do to hold back the tears. "How much money do you have, Michele?"

I figured that with the money I had left, and the little Michele had, we might be able to hire a taxi to take us back to the spot where we could catch the bus. I called a cab from the pay phone outside the building.

A gruff looking man with the usual facial hair that goes along with not showering for about a month picked us up. The inside of his cab wasn't much better. It smelled of dirty grease and drool. The cushions were ripped, the door handle dangled, half of it unattached, and the seat belts didn't function. When we got to the spot where we had exited the bus, I told him, "You can let us out here."

He turned and looked at us over his shoulder. "I'm not letting you girls out here."

I looked at Michele and swallowed hard. What was he going to do with us? I could not believe what I had gotten us into.

The cabby explained, "You girls wouldn't last ten minutes on that corner."

I looked at that corner where we had stood for almost half an hour on our way to the arena and realized the woman who had stood next to us, had been watching over us.

"We don't have any more money," I explained.

He turned off his meter. "That's okay. I could not live with myself if I let you out here. Where do you need to go?"

He drove us all the way back to Thompson-Markward Hall.

I learned a valuable lesson that day. There are a lot of good people in this world, and many of them are not Mormons. I also learned the Lord was watching over me. And as the stranger we met on Pennsylvania Avenue warned, I needed to watch my step.

7

NASTY RUNS AND CRANKY PEOPLE

Security was not the only matter where I received help from the whisperings of the Spirit while I was in Washington. Days after Michele returned to Salt Lake, Thompson-Markward Hall buzzed with the news there would be a party that night in Georgetown. Turns out a student at the university had been a page the year before, and she still had contact with some of the pages who had stayed on another year.

I didn't care about the party, but I couldn't wait to see Georgetown. I loved the epic feel of Washington, D.C., the sense that every step touched some historic story. I also loved the architecture of the grand neighborhoods, especially the winding roads around the numerous embassies. And just as I expected, I loved Georgetown. The narrow cobblestone paved roads formed a network of avenues between quaint, brick, row houses. An occasional polished brass plaque noted where some important figure once lived. Had I been alone, I would have taken the time to read each one and basked in the honor of touching each doorknob. But as it was, the former page led us like ducklings from the bus stop, over the now darkened cobblestones, to one of the dorm halls at Georgetown University.

✗ As I crossed the threshold, the Spirit whispered, "Make your decision now, and you will never have to make it again." This sounded oddly familiar, like a lesson at Church. I connected those words to the advice given in the lesson: if you make a decision about what you will do before a situation arises, then when you are faced with temptation, the decision has already been made. I soon understood why the Spirit warned me.

"Everybody sit down in a circle," the former page told us. Some Georgetown students meandered in and joined the circle.

Trent Farnsworth stared at me. He was one of the page overseers who assigned us our errands throughout the day. If he liked you, he gave you easy runs to fun offices and then brought you back to the House Floor where you could visit with him and the other pages, watch Congress in action, or go on personal errands for the Congressmen. If Trent didn't like you, he gave you nasty runs through tunnels to dingy offices with cranky people and he kept you out running for the whole day, rarely bringing you back.

I don't think Trent hated me, but I don't think he liked me much either. He knew I was Mormon, and since he was Catholic, he wasn't too impressed. He was also trim, blonde, very good looking, and carried an air of confidence that made him seem important.

The former page pulled out a bottle of whiskey and a shot glass. Everyone in the circle oohed and aahed as though they had just witnessed a fireworks display. The game started directly across from me, and one by one, each person took his or her turn swallowing a shot of whiskey before passing it to the next person. As each one finished, the bottle moved closer to me, and my heart started beating faster. Leaving was not an option. I didn't know the way home, and going anywhere alone at night wasn't safe. Plus I didn't have much money.

Maybe you're asking, why is drinking such a big deal to Mormons? After all, I was there in Washington, far away from home. Nobody knew me. If I did drink this once, no one would know. And if I didn't participate, they'd probably all hate me and write me off as a prude or a goody-goody.

By way of explanation, members of The Church of Jesus Christ of Latter-day Saints believe in a revelation given to the Prophet Joseph Smith, which is recorded in the book called the Doctrine and Covenants and is called the Word of Wisdom. It is a health code that makes promises to Church members who abstain from using coffee, tea, and alcohol. It is a principle with a promise, since obedience results in these specific blessings: "And all saints who remember to keep and do these sayings, walking in obedience to the commandments, shall receive health in their navel and marrow to their bones; And shall find wisdom and great treasures of knowledge, even hidden treasures; And shall run and not be weary, and shall walk and not faint. And I, the Lord, give unto them a promise, that the destroying angel shall pass by them, as the children of Israel, and not slay them" (D&C 89:18-21). To me, a choice not to drink was a covenant with God. That's why it meant so much to me.

Trent stared at me again. The bottle was next to me. "It's your turn," Trent announced, emphasizing *your*.

— I took the bottle and tried to hand it to the next person.

— "You can't pass!" Trent shouted.

— I kind of smiled, "Okay. Where's the water?" I stood up and ran over to a drinking fountain and filled the shot glass, and when I was back in the circle, I swigged it down like whiskey, giving out a loud "ahhh," then passed the jug and glass on to the next person. I took in a deep breath before looking back over at Trent. He rolled his eyes in disgust.

For the next several months, I took my runs through tunnels to dingy offices with cranky people and rarely returned to the House floor unless the day was over. But, I enjoyed it. I learned to love being with myself while exploring the underbelly and catacombs of those mysterious buildings. I made up games for myself, such as how many runs I could do in one day, or how far I could travel. It didn't hurt that I also lost about thirty pounds along with all the baby fat I'd been desperate to be rid of. I also made a study of cranky people. Their faces looked permanently pinched, and no matter what they said or how they said it, their voices sounded sour. I decided I never wanted to be cranky.

I'm glad now that every time I called in to the page desk to get my next run, and Trent Farnsworth gave me the nastiest run of the century, I didn't complain. I'm glad I didn't whine or feel sorry for myself for several reasons. First of all, after Trent's tenure was up at Christmas, he left for home. I guess Mr. Oliver, the head guy in charge of all the pages, had pity and gave me Trent's job as one of the page overseers. My running days were over. And it was true, after I made my decision that night in Georgetown to be true to who I was, I never had to make the choice again for the rest of my time in Washington. But the most important reason—I had no idea how much I would need those blessings that come from obedience to the Word of Wisdom. Those promises would play a more important role in my life than I could ever imagine.

THE AFTERMATH

I spent my entire senior year there in Washington, D.C., and attended the Capitol Page School (CPS) in the Library of Congress. I have fond memories of watching the sun rise every morning from the school windows there on the top floor. The secretary, Mrs. Williams, was our southern mother. Mr. Balducci taught English, and Mr. McGrath taught history. He is probably still lamenting our independence from the British Empire. I graduated from CPS in June of 1980 and received my high school diploma from President Jimmy Carter there in the East Room at the White House.

During the ceremony, I was seated on the aisle on the third row. A huge thrill swept through me when President Carter walked into the room. After all, he was the President of the United States. He looked more weighted down and older than I imagined. When I shook his hand, he asked me, "Where are you from?" Luckily, I remembered. After the ceremony, they had refreshments for us in the State Room and we were allowed to wander in all of the rooms open to the public.

I made many discoveries about myself during my time in Washington. In November of 1979, I recorded in my journal that my mission in life was to make others feel good about themselves. I returned to this theme over and over throughout the year, especially in times of struggle. I'm not sure I succeeded, but I did come to some important realizations that would affect the rest of my life.

After Christmas, I moved out of Thompson-Markward Hall and moved into an apartment with four other pages. Lonnie from Illinois was short with a happy face. She would eat breakfast and with each bite say, "This is today's lunch…" then "this is tonight's dinner …" By the time she had consumed one piece of toast, she had eaten her entire week of food.

Mindy from Pennsylvania was blonde and attractive. She was Miss Teen USA, student body president of her high school back home, and a model, among other amazing accomplishments. We believed all of this until Lonnie found some pictures. Mindy was actually Miss Trailer Queen of her family's camping organization. Mindy was, however, having an affair with one of the page managers. This truth was just one more relationship uncovered in the page scandal of that year. We already knew. The fact that a car picked her up every night around 3:00 A.M. had been our first clue.

Rhonda had big dark eyes, perfect skin, and long, wavy black hair. Though she was beautiful, she was all business. She had a plan for her life and was not going to be dependent on any man. I admired her determination.

Bridget from Ohio was wickedly fun. She did impressions of everyone from pages to Congressmen. Her naturally high voice made it even funnier. She was also the one with the bright idea to make brownies for the boys at Mr. Oliver's, and lace them with laxatives. And on any given day, she would order them random taxis or pizzas. On a few occasions, they returned the favor by calling for us unnecessary repairmen and tow trucks.

We lived in an upstairs apartment on 313 Third Street, N.E., right next to the Green Street Bar. Every night we were wakened at 2:00 A.M. as the owners threw their empty liquor bottles into the dumpster under our window. We rented furniture for the living room but slept with our mattresses on the floor in the two bedrooms upstairs. A little, elderly lady who lived in the basement rented us the apartment.

When my roommates turned up their music or invited other pages over for parties, I'd constantly tell them to be quiet "because of the little lady downstairs." They were irritated. I finally learned to leave and go somewhere else so I wouldn't worry so much about that poor woman below us. On one occasion, we made cookies to take to her as a peace offering— only to find she was diabetic.

I wanted good things for my roommates and knowing you "reap what you sow," along with my sense of accountability, I encouraged them to choose the right and not be too mean to some of the other pages. I'm sure I made lots of other "encouraging" comments as well. I had their best interests at heart, but these comments might not have come out or been received exactly the way I intended.

Bridget and I were the best of friends. But where I was quiet and reserved, Bridget was loud, used her entire body when she talked, and had an endearing laugh. I tried to be kind, but Bridget had a million comebacks and constantly thought of pranks to pull on everyone. Over time, I learned to love going out in public with her and watching everyone's reactions to her animated conversations. I even went to visit her in her hometown when our tenure was over. We kept in touch through college until she stopped writing. When I attended an informal 10-year page reunion back in Washington, Bridget was cold and indifferent. I asked her, "What happened?" She was brutally honest.

She told me that she and Rhonda had also kept in touch. Though I did not realize it while I was in Washington, Rhonda despised me. When she and Bridget talked, Rhonda referred to me as the "Guilt Queen." I don't think it helped that Rhonda dated Jake Tyler, and Jake and I were good friends. He worked in the cloakroom right by my desk, and we often talked about what it meant to be a Mormon, including the strict moral standards. It also didn't help that Jake knew I had never been kissed and made it his personal goal to make sure I didn't make it to "Sweet 18" without initiating me. Rhonda didn't have anything to worry about; she was gorgeous. But over the years, Rhonda converted Bridget, until Bridget didn't want anything to do with me.

I appreciated Bridget's honesty.

I've given this feedback serious thought since then. I realize I was giving them unwanted messages. If I had not loved them, perhaps I could have stood by and said nothing. Or if I had been more cynical, I would have understood some in the world consider pleasure worth any consequence. But I was hopelessly naïve and acted too much like a parent. I'm grateful to Bridget for letting me know.

But beyond that, this was the first time I understood that though we are all humans and share so many universal characteristics, we are individuals. Each one of us views the world from our own eyes affected by years of relationships, experiences, and perceptions. We all have unique personalities with differing strengths and weaknesses. How narrow-minded of me to expect others to react the way I reacted, or to see the world the way I saw it when these traits were unique to me. They had a right to live their own lives. Their different hearts would lead them in a different direction. Who was I to tell them what they should do?

This understanding draws me to others now. I love uncovering the mysteries of each person I meet and learning to appreciate the world through his or her eyes. The stories they share widen my view, and I benefit from the wisdom they've gained without having to endure the trial. I have come to understand that regardless of circumstances or appearances, we are all doing our best. This was the gift of Bridget's honesty. I wish I had learned it earlier.

I can't help but wonder how the years have treated these friends from Washington? What discoveries have they made about their lives and choices? I often think of them and send my love for them into the universe.

And for the record, I did not make it un-kissed to sweet 18. On one of our last nights in Washington, we had a page dance. Jake Tyler had always teased about giving me a "big, wet kiss" before we left, so before the dance was over, he pulled me out into the hall and led me down an escalator shaft.

I did want to kiss him. He was gorgeous, and I adored him, but I worried about Rhonda. Jake put my fears to rest when he assured me, "This is a 'friend kiss,' ML, not a 'lover's kiss'."

We were such good friends. I wasn't even embarrassed to tell him, "Jake, I am so scared."

He was good about it. He laughed and said, "One, two, three . . ."

I responded pathetically. I felt so bad about giving him such a bad kiss, I gave him a hug instead.

"Now, ML, this is our secret. We can't tell anyone."

(Now that it's been thirty years and he didn't end up marrying Rhonda anyway, I figure it's okay to mention it. But just in case, I did change his name. In fact, I changed all their names.)

9

STUMBLING BLOCKS

While my co-Salutatorian from Capitol Page School attended Princeton and many of my other friends from our graduating class attended other prestigious Ivy League colleges, I returned home to help take care of Mom and attend the University of Utah. This was 1980, the year Ronald Reagan was elected president of the United States, Mount St. Helen erupted, and the US Hockey Team defeated the Russians in the Winter Olympics. I came home to find Susan having a difficult time dealing with the stress of taking care of Mom and having Rob home from his mission. He was going through a difficult adjustment himself. Sue had decided that when I arrived home, it was time for her to leave again. She moved to Provo to attend BYU.

Although the University of Utah was not Harvard, I knew that with the load of responsibilities I carried at home, I would need help to be successful in my classes. A friend of mine, who was a year older, told me how she had made a covenant with the Lord. She promised to read her scriptures every day and asked for His help with her schooling in return.

This friend bore such a strong testimony of how this had blessed her life, I decided to try it for myself.

While I was in college, I read my scriptures every day for at least fifteen minutes. I would love to say this made life easy for me, everything went smoothly, and I never had any problems. The truth is I struggled.

I left a situation in Washington where I lived a selfish life. At home, Mom's care required huge demands, especially as we no longer had Veda and all of the household chores were left to me. Mom also expected me to cook for Rob and pay for his groceries. In addition, we had financial concerns. Mom was running out of money. We looked into moving and had an offer pending on our house, but it fell through. In the end, Rob and I used the Social Security benefits we received from Dad's death to pay for our household expenses. Fortunately, we both had scholarships to cover the cost of our education.

My belief in God, religion, and the Mormon Church also suffered. I stumbled through bouts of discouragement. Why did my life have to be so hard? Many of my professors at the University also made it their goal to undermine faith. They knew they had a predominantly Mormon audience and a majority of their lecture time was devoted to preaching an alternate truth. In their eyes, organized religion was simply another vehicle to extort money and power and any pretense of spirituality was irrelevant. I spent a great deal of time sorting out my own religious reality.

I agonized over what was to become of me and my life. Who was I supposed to be and what was I supposed to do? My declared major when I began at the University was fuels engineering. I wanted to discover new fuel sources. I spent a year in science courses and calculus.

During this time, I also had a serious relationship. He was a returned missionary and my first true love. We dated for seven months and came to the point of deciding whether or not to get married. On the night when we both agreed to fast and pray about it, about a month after Prince Charles had married

Princess Diana, my boyfriend told me, "Let's have the courage to do what's right. Let's have the courage to trust the Lord's decision, whether it be 'yes,' or 'no'."

I never did receive a positive answer. Neither did he. Within the month, we had broken up. I later received a letter from him in which he said, "Our lives have gone in different paths," I wrote in my journal. "I guess it was pretty hard to take, but you know, I've got to respect that. I still care about him and I think I always will. That doesn't mean I want to date him again, but it does mean that I want him to be happy. Oh, well, I hope this is the last of that." That seemingly matter-of-fact summary does not adequately convey the devastating pain of that loss.

I had to be my own best friend. There were nights when I would think about being a mother and having a daughter. If she were going through this, what would I tell her? It helped me to distance myself from the situation and see it from another perspective. I was only nineteen.

Through it all, I did read my scriptures. Like anything, you never really know how it's affected you, or what your life would have been like otherwise, but all along the way, little things happened.

There was a feeling that came with reading the scriptures that gave me strength. Despite the negative situation I lived in and the negativity of the people around me, I determined I would be positive. That feeling I received from reading the scriptures was my incentive.

The stories in the scriptures, particularly The Book of Mormon, also gave me comfort. I didn't read about perfect people who had perfect lives. I read about good people who tried really hard and things didn't always go the way they planned either. And God still loved them. I read about believers who defended their faith under trying and threatening circumstances. In every case, they prevailed. They overcame their challenges, or died in peace knowing they were true to themselves and to God. I felt their strength.

And when I had questions about my life, people seemed to show up at just the right time to give me the direction I needed. Rick (Richard) Eyre was my Sunday School teacher. His wife, Linda, had been my Young Women leader. Rick taught me about setting goals and the importance of envisioning the kind of person I wanted to be. I gave this a lot of thought and wrote at that time:

"ML Schoenhals: She is a very understanding, tolerant, forgiving, supportive, helpful, active, enjoyable, cheerful, interesting, and consistent person. She is also very serene. She shies away from being dominant but is very diligent in doing what she thinks is right. She is very close to the Spirit. She finds comfort and joy in the knowledge of the truth. She seeks the guidance of the Spirit daily and acts in accordance with inspiration received. She is a friend to all, and people seek her company. She has worked and achieved a unified family so that she can feel a sense of peace and calm when viewing her stewardships. She can look forward to death with a feeling of dignity, accomplishment, and joy; for she has done those things she has been sent here to do."

Under my "Clarifying Statements of my Personal Values," I included this one: "Be cheerful and bear adversity well: I do not complain of physical ailments. I do not burden others with my problems but seek to lighten theirs. I am happy and look forward to every moment with great anticipation. I see the positive and bright side of every situation. I don't complain – I do something about it. I know there is something to learn from every mishap or misfortune."

Though I wrote these thoughts when I was only nineteen, these visions have greatly impacted my life.

On another occasion, I was irritated. I had to interrupt my day and run home from school for an appointment with my visiting teachers. This is a program in the Church where every female is assigned two women to visit her every month. The idea is to meet the individual needs of the members and to make sure everyone has a friend. What could these women, who were both my mother's age, possibly do for me? As we talked, they asked me about my plans for the future. I told them I wasn't sure what I should do. Sister Robison asked, "Have you ever considered getting a nursing degree?"

I never had. But that was the answer I had been searching for. This happened about the same time as my relationship with the young man I mentioned earlier ended. I would better understand the significance of this later, but he was right. Our paths had gone in different directions.

The one reason I had covenanted with the Lord to read my scriptures was to receive help with my schooling. He certainly kept His end of the bargain. I had so many fortuitous experiences, I could never do justice to the help I received. But to give you one example, I was taking the third and most difficult chemistry course, Biochemistry. It was the last of the prerequisites I needed before I could apply to nursing school. The class was huge; I was one of three hundred students, including premed majors. We met in a large lecture hall, and the professor was young and talked with an intense cadence. We'd taken a test and he was passing out our results. After all the exams were returned, he asked in front of everyone, "Is ML Schoenhals here?"

I raised my hand.

"I want to speak with you after class."

I couldn't imagine why he wanted to see me. After the lecture, I walked into his office and told him who I was.

"Can you explain to me," he asked, "how you got a 97 on this exam and the next closest score was a 73?"

It didn't even occur to me at the time, that he thought I might have cheated. I just shook my head and shrugged my shoulders. "I studied for the exam."

He gave a big sigh. "You can go."

As I walked away from his office, I knew why I had done so well. The day I took that test, I looked at each problem and knew immediately how to solve it. The answers came easily and I knew when they were right. I had to show all my work, so the

49

professor must have known I understood the material. But there was really only one explanation as to why I had done so well. It was the same in every class all through college. God didn't just help me, He carried me.

While I grew more dependent on Him, many others in that university environment fell away. It seemed to change everything about them. Their spiritual unwinding changed the way they looked, how they spoke, dressed, everything. It completely transformed them into someone less—less attractive, less refined, and less considerate. I took a psychology class where they identified the various components of a human being as though they were slicing up a pie: the physical, emotional, cognitive, spiritual, etc. Conceptually it was true; we do have different aspects to who we are, but I could see not all of these pieces were equally weighted.

On one hand, here was my mom whose "physical" aspect was devastated, and yet she functioned. Although not "religious," she was deeply moral. She had a strong character and sense of presence. For those who lost their spiritual center, the change to them as a person seemed far more dramatic.

This scared me. I knew I was not immune to spiritual crises. I remember one night telling my Father in Heaven, "Please, I give you permission to do whatever you need to, to keep me close. I am asking you to never let me fall away. Please promise me you will keep me close."

So many times when I look back at my life and what I have experienced, I realize He was keeping His promise.

10

Nursing 180

My first nursing class was Nursing 180, which met in the nursing building on upper campus next to the University Hospital. The long room flooded with 200 anxious students, 197 of them girls. Two of my sorority sisters were in the class, and they happened to be two of the wildest, party-loving women I knew. Although we did not share similar interests, I adored their entertaining personalities. They also happened to know one of the three boys taking the class and sat by him every day. They all seemed to be very good friends. For a boy going into nursing at that time, he seemed normal and was a nice looking, outgoing guy. Realizing one of my "sisters" was interested in the boy and wouldn't appreciate my moving in on her territory, I purposely sat on the end of our little group, as far away from him as possible.

Getting to this class was a challenge. After my class ended on lower campus, I had to hike back to my car in a distant parking lot then drive to the nursing building on the upper campus where there was rarely an open parking space. I had to do all of this in ten minutes. On one particular day, a series of miracles happened and I found close parking spaces on both the

51

lower campus and at the nursing school. Since I was early, I sat down on a couch outside the classroom in a lobby area. It just so happened, the boy who was close friends with my sorority sisters also showed up. Although we'd been in the same class for several weeks, this was the first time I had spoken to him.

We talked about the reason he wanted to go into nursing. He was interested in medical sales and had met with some medical equipment companies. He had been told that if he would get his nursing degree, they would start him at double the salary. At one point in the conversation, he mentioned he had gone on a mission. I know, I had lived in Salt Lake, and had been a member of the Mormon Church my entire life, but given the type of girls he hung out with I had to ask, "For what church?"

He busted out laughing. "What church do you think? The Mormon Church."

"Oh, okay." Now I was totally confused.

We made small talk until class started, and I was careful once again to sit on the other end from where he sat. It continued this way throughout the rest of the quarter. On the last day of the class, he sat next to me for the final exam. I thought this was so odd. There were plenty of other seats open, including some closer to my sorority sisters. The only possible reason I could come up with that he would want to sit by me was so he could cheat off my test.

After the exam was over, he leaned close, "Can I have your phone number?"

Why on earth would he want my number? I knew he loved to hang-glide, and when we talked that one day, I had mentioned how fun it must be.

I gave him my number and said, "I'd love to see you hang-glide sometime."

I walked away baffled. Why would he want my number? I was not the type of girl boys wanted to take out. My sorority sisters were. I wasn't fun. I didn't laugh and make jokes. My life was sober and serious.

Oh, well. I figured I wouldn't have to worry about it. I gave myself a one in ten chance he would ever call anyway. His name was Kent Pearson.

Within the week, however, Kent called. It turned out his sister, Ann, was in my ward, the local unit of my church. A new subdivision had been built in the fields behind my house, and I didn't know all of the new families that had moved in. He was staying at his sister's house while she was out of town, around the corner from me, and would I like to come over and go swimming in her pool? I accepted his invitation and we decided to buy some food from the store to cook for dinner.

As we walked through the grocery store, all the employees greeted me as an old friend, asking, "ML, how did your finals go?"

On the way back to his sister's house, he asked me, "How do all of those people know you?"

I had to think for a minute. I'd been shopping there since I was fifteen or sixteen, about four years, and hadn't realized myself I'd become so familiar with all the employees. I told him, "That's where I do our grocery shopping." The uniqueness of my situation and responsibilities at home did not even cross my mind.

That night, Kent told me his life story. He told me about all the mistakes he'd made and all the cars he'd crashed. For the first time, I actually looked at him. He had sincere, dark brown eyes and hints of freckles on his cheeks. He wore his thick auburn hair just long enough for the waves to lift off his ears. His smile gave him a mischievous look, especially with his cleft chin. But he was fun. He had confidence, and he loved to talk.

When I arrived home after my date, Rob asked me, "How was it?"

"That was one of the most fun dates I've ever been on, but I don't think I'd ever want to marry the guy." I still wasn't certain what he was really like.

Kent and I spent a lot of time together while he was staying at his sister's. On one occasion, I stopped by the Delta

Gamma house to see the sorority sister who liked him. They were taking an anatomy class together that quarter. I wondered if Kent had said anything to her about me. I wasn't sure how to bring up the subject, so I simply asked, "How's Kent doing?" When she told me about all their time together in class and how they studied together, I figured Kent hadn't mentioned a word. I couldn't help it, I left so curious why he would be such good friends and spend so much time with this girl when she made a point of telling everyone how much she loved to party, and he was a returned missionary. Generally, returned missionaries lived pretty sober lives. Who was Kent really? Was he one of those people who changed depending on who he was with?

One day Kent laughed at me for questioning which church he'd served a mission for. It was my chance. "I'm sure you must have thought I was nuts, but given the self-acknowledged party animals you hang out with, I didn't want to assume anything."

"Oh." He nodded. "Your friend likes me, you know that don't you? Whenever we study, she likes to say, 'It's a study date, right?' Let's face it, she's an incredibly fun girl, with a fun personality, but she's not the kind of person I would date."

As I got to know him better, I noticed his willingness to talk to anyone and be a friend to everyone, regardless of their beliefs. He had a way of making people feel important, and they loved him. He had a quick wit with an endearing, self-deprecating humor. And he seemed to enjoy being with me. On one occasion he said to me again, "Your friend likes me." He was referring to another sorority sister, also in nursing.

I chided him, "You think everyone's in love with you. She knows we're dating."

He shrugged. "I'm just warning you."

That evening, this "friend" called Kent up asking him for a ride home from the airport. "Oh, yes," he told her, "We'll be right out."

He took me with him to pick her up. Needless to say, he made his point with her, and with me. He knew how to read people, what motivated them, what upset them, and how to work with them. The more I watched, the more I recognized he had a gift. He had a lot of friends from all walks of life, and many of them considered Kent their "best friend." I was relieved to see that no matter whom he was with, he was true to his ideals and never pretended to be something or someone he wasn't.

Another trait that softened my heart toward him was his sensitivity to my situation. From that first date when he asked how I knew everyone in the grocery store, he constantly supported me. He seemed to genuinely want to make my life easier. After we had dated for several months he wrote me a letter, ". . . ML, I really love you with all my heart, and always know I will do anything for you that I can. Please always know that you can call on me when you need help for anything . . ."

I could never accuse Kent of beating around the bush. One night when we were together and I was contemplating my upcoming twenty-first birthday (the age at which LDS women are eligible to serve full-time missions) I mentioned, "I think it would be so exciting to serve a mission."

Kent pulled the car over to the shoulder of the road and stopped. He turned and looked at me, pausing to make sure he had my full attention. "If you ever decide you'd like to serve a mission, be sure to let me know so we can stop dating. I'm going to be turning twenty-five, and I'm not dating just to be dating. I'm dating to get married."

I never brought up a mission again. We did talk about marriage. Not so much about us getting married, but about marriage in general.

During this time, my brother, Rob, started complaining of feeling dizzy. He'd been waterskiing with some friends and had taken a bad fall. When the symptoms persisted, he went in for a CAT scan. The next thing we knew, Rob was having brain surgery. Oddly enough, the tumor was in the same location as Mom's had been. Just as a precaution, the neurosurgeon recommended Sue and I also have a CAT scan. Both of us had the scan, but ours were normal.

The night following my exam, as Kent was dropping me off, he made the comment, "ML, even if you had a brain tumor, I would still love you. I would still want to marry you." I did not realize at that time, the profound implications of his declaration. We had been dating for about a year.

As my twenty-first birthday approached, Kent made plans to celebrate by cooking breakfast up Millcreek, one of the canyons east of Salt Lake City. That week, as I was saying my prayers, I had an overwhelming feeling come over me, as if I were receiving a spiritual message. It said, and I quote, "If you married Kent, it would be a good thing." I had never experienced anything like that before. I wasn't even praying about whether or not I should marry Kent. I soon understood why I had that prompting.

During our breakfast up Millcreek Canyon, as Kent was starting the barbeque to cook our pancakes, he asked me to go and get the spatula out of his car. When I opened the trunk, there was the spatula, along with a beautiful, solitaire diamond ring in a velvet blue box. I picked up the spatula and closed the trunk.

Stunned, I walked down and handed Kent the spatula. "I think there was something else in there I wasn't supposed to see."

He smiled and gave me a big hug. "Will you marry me, ML?"

How grateful I was I had already received my answer. If ever I had doubted, I knew that minute God knew me. He knew what was going on in my life. He knew what I needed. All my life I had been taught I had to ask in order to receive. This was the first time I realized there are times when God also enjoys giving without having to be asked. And Kent was a wonderful gift.

11

CLEAVING

Getting engaged was easy. The engagement itself, well, that was a little more complicated. While growing up, I hadn't given any thought about what to do about my mother in the event that I should marry. I hadn't even considered there would be a change in our relationship. Though physically dependent, Mom had a bright mind and was capable of making responsible decisions. She was the adult, I was the child. I always figured that when it was time for me to leave, she would make the necessary arrangements to meet her own needs. I don't think either she or I realized the depth or breadth of her dependence on me.

As my relationship with Kent progressed, Mom knew our situation would change. To her credit, she never discouraged me or interfered. On only one occasion did she say anything negative about him, when she said, "That Kent has kind of a mean streak in him, but if things don't work out with him, he sure has a nice brother." (She was referring to Kent's younger brother, Steve, whom she had met on several occasions.)

By this time, Sue had finished her year at BYU, married, and moved with her new husband to Winnemucca, Nevada.

As my relationship with Kent continued, Mom made the decision to sell her home and buy a condo in Bountiful, Utah, closer to her family. Now she would put the oft repeated slogan of her sisters and mother, "If only you lived closer, we could help," to the test. (And they did in fact prove their love and devotion with daily visits as long as Mom lived there in Bountiful.) Mom remodeled the unit she purchased, made all the decisions regarding the decorating, and arranged to have everything boxed up and moved.

Kent and I often discussed my mother and her situation. I know it was not a coincidence that Kent had grown up with his maternal grandmother living in his home. He had witnessed years of his grandmother insisting on sitting in the front seat of the car and expecting that Betty, Kent's mother, meet her needs at the expense of her husband and children. Though physically able, Kent's grandmother was not emotionally healthy. The toll her demands had taken could easily be seen in the family dynamics. I'm sure there were many reasons, but Kent attributed much of this to the strain of having a mother-in-law in the home. Kent was adamant. If we were to marry, he would come before my mother.

He constantly reminded me I had a brother and sister and, if necessary, they would need to do their share. In his own situation, his mother also had a brother and a sister, but other than visiting occasionally, they did not participate in the day-to-day care of his grandmother. Kent was certain his aunt and uncle were both willing and had offered to help, but for reasons Kent was not privy to, his mother remained the sole caregiver. To Kent's dismay, his grandmother often talked of his aunt and uncle and how wonderful they were without saying anything positive about Kent's mother or father, the ones who cared for her on a daily basis. Kent had no intention of seeing this cycle repeated in his own family.

In the year and a half Kent and I dated, I witnessed his concerns first-hand. I did not want this for my family either. And yet, I loved my mom. I enjoyed doing things for her, and I enjoyed being with her. But I knew I had to pull back. It did not help that Mom's abilities continued to fail. Where before she could get out of bed, and use her walker to get to the bathroom on her own, now she needed help just to sit up in bed. She needed someone to help lift so she could stand. She felt more comfortable with someone beside her as she used her walker. This was certainly warranted. On two occasions before the move to Bountiful, she had fallen. Because of her brain surgeries, the back of her head had no skull for protection. For several hours after each fall she asked me the same questions over and over. I was grateful I was in nursing and had some training in how to care for people. I watched her closely for other signs of a serious head injury but was relieved on both occasions when she recovered without any residual effects. She couldn't go to the bathroom by herself either. She needed help sitting down, and help standing up.

I had two part-time jobs so Kent and I could afford to be married. One day while at work, Rob called me. "You need to come home and take Mom to the bathroom."

"I can't come home, I'm at work." I knew all that was needed was to simply help Mom sit and then stand again when she finished. Rob was right there and could even do it with his eyes closed.

"You need to come home right now to take Mom to the bathroom. She needs to go."

That was the moment I knew how much Mom depended on me. I did not go home. If she was not willing to let Rob help, or he was not willing to help her, they would need to find another way. I was not going to be there much longer. How would she go to the bathroom after I was married?

This incident upset Mom. That night as I stood by her so she could walk the short distance from her living room to her bedroom with her walker, she fumed, "You don't think of anyone but yourself."

"Mom, I am in school full-time, I have two part-time jobs, and I am engaged to be married. I also happen to be the

Delta Gamma Rush Chairman." (Rush is the process where university students decide which fraternity or sorority they want to join, and it is a huge undertaking that requires lots of time and effort.)

Mom's gait faltered and she leaned perilously to one side. I steadied her walker so she didn't tip over. "But how thoughtless of you to take all of that on."

"The only reason I joined a sorority, Mom, is because you insisted. It was important to you that I be in a sorority. They've asked me to be the Rush Chairman, and you are the one who has always told me to follow through on my responsibilities. What would you like me to do? As soon as rush is over, I'm getting married. We need to figure this out, Mom. We've got to find someone to help you."

A tear dropped onto her walker. Her jaw tightened, and she pounded the walker into the floor as she moved toward her bed. "Just move out then."

She and I both knew that given her condition, and how dependent she was on me, I would never "just move out." But as her needs increased, and my responsibilities did as well, there were more incidents and more frustrations. Mom finally got to the point where she would call Aunt Joyce or Nanny. I know they were happy to help Mom, so it was probably my own guilt that made it feel as if they were saying, "if you would just do your job . . . " whenever they had to come over. I felt awful. And I ached for Mom and her continuing loss of function.

I understood Mom didn't like asking other people for help. I knew her routine, anticipated her needs, and made it possible for her to maintain a sense of dignity and independence. I tried to be pleasant and willing to help. I wish I could have helped her understand it wasn't about me and I wanted her to have what she needed. I wish we could have discussed what arrangements could be made to help her, but we could never get beyond how ungrateful and selfish I was for not being there when she needed me.

The extended family reinforced this. On one occasion, Nanny commented to me, "I'm surprised you're going into nursing since you don't have much of a caring or a compassionate nature."

Kent often took me aside, wishing there was a way to get me out of there sooner. It reminded him too much of his own mother and how she was treated by his grandmother.

But I knew most of Mom's frustrations came from the loss of her body's function. For some reason, she could not talk about what was happening to her physically. She never expressed fear about her future or complained about her condition. Not one word! Mom had to have been terrified and upset about what was happening to her body. I had learned in my nursing classes that sick people only get angry with those they trust. I also understood that Mom's complaining to Nanny and Aunt Joyce about my inadequacies was, in her mind, an acceptable way to vent some of her frustration, even if I was a misplaced target. I did not take their treatment as personally as Kent did. And perhaps Nanny was right; maybe the reason I needed to go into nursing was so I could learn those nurturing qualities most people developed naturally from having a healthy and attentive mother. And for Mom's sake, I was grateful she had such loyal and supportive advocates as Nanny and Aunt Joyce.

Since I had to get rush over with first, and then the quarter started, it made more sense to wait until the Christmas break to get married. That would make our engagement six months, but would give me additional time to work out the situation with my mom.

Before the fall quarter started, I was up to my eyeballs with rush, sanding Delta Gamma anchors, along with taking care of a million other little details. I would never have joined a sorority, but Mom was the one who wanted me to go through rush as a freshman. She had been a Pi Phi and insisted I join a sorority. While I was away preparing for rush, Mom had another unmet need. When I arrived home to her frustration and refrain of "Just move out then," I finally caved in. I knew things were only going to get worse.

"Okay, Mom, I'll move out." I packed up my stuff and moved into the Delta Gamma Sorority house, grateful for a place to go.

After moving out, I spent a great deal of time at night thinking. Having spent almost my whole life helping Mom, couldn't things have turned out a little better? My relationship with her always felt unfinished; more like a frayed edge than a smooth seam. What could I have done differently? Into my mind came a picture of Kent's mom—a daughter in her 50s still trying to please her own mother every day, always falling short despite her willingness to sacrifice everything. If I had sacrificed school, work, Kent, and everything else, would my relationship with Mom be any different? I realized I could never please my mom, either. No matter what I gave up or how many years I stayed with her, she would always see me as selfish and ungrateful. I would never be able to change the minds of my aunts and grandmother either. Though I would always love my mother and do what I could to help her, the time had come for me to move forward in a new direction.

The confirmation that I should marry Kent bore deeper into my soul. God wanted me to marry. He wanted me to have a life. And in giving me Kent, along with his family, God had given me a vision of my own situation from another perspective. There in my bunk at the Delta Gamma Sorority house, I was at peace. At that time in my life, I was where I needed to be.

I had a wonderful man who loved me. He understood my dilemma and validated my struggle. He constantly talked of wanting to make my life happy. And we were engaged to be married in the temple of God.

Several weeks before I went to the temple, as I was preparing to make personal covenants with God, I wrote, "I am so looking forward to going to the temple. I hope that I am ready and prepared so that it will be a special and meaningful experience. I hope that it will accomplish a few things too—

bring Kent's parents closer together, bring my family closer together, let everyone know I'm not such a bad kid after all, and bring me closer to my Father in Heaven. I really want to work on getting to know Him."

It just so happened, that after a few weeks of relying on Rob, Aunt Joyce, and Nanny, Mom found a full-time helper. Since I was gone, this sweet woman was able to move into my room and be available to help Mom twenty-four hours a day.

This experience gave me a new understanding of the word *cleave* as it relates to marriage. It is the only word I know that has two completely opposite meanings. On the one hand, "cleave" means to split, or to separate into distinct parts. But on the other, it also means to join together—firmly, closely, and loyally. In the circumstances of my own marriage, both definitions applied.

12

SEALING

I received my endowment in the Salt Lake Temple on December 14, 1983. The ceremonies that take place in the temple are sacred and are not discussed in any detail outside of those holy edifices. But generally speaking, the temple endowment is a gift from God to an individual Church member, which involves making covenants with the Lord in return for a greater understanding of how to successfully prepare to receive eternal life. In a sense, the temple serves as earth's access to heaven. To prepare for this important event in my life, I took classes to better understand the nature of the covenants I would make and the significance of our temple marriage or "sealing."

Throughout history, God's covenant people have been commanded to build temples. In the New Testament, the Savior said to Peter, "I will give unto thee the keys of the kingdom of heaven: and whatsoever thou shalt bind on earth shall be bound in heaven" (Matthew 16:19). I believed then as I do now that those who officiate in the temple hold those keys today, and through the temple ordinances, Kent and I would be bound together forever, as we would also be bound to God.

I had already felt that eternal power and promise when I was sealed to my mother and father by proxy after my father's death, but this time I would be receiving these ordinances for myself. This experience would be a little different.

First of all, the temple is a holy place. No unclean thing should enter, and, therefore, I had to be worthy. This included being morally clean, honest in my dealings with men and in my dealings with God through my payment of tithes, remaining physically clean by abstaining from the use of harmful or addictive substances, and by keeping the Word of Wisdom. I also needed to have a sincere belief in God and His power and believe that these keys of the kingdom had been restored to earth in these last days for the salvation of all mankind. And was I willing and prepared to make eternal covenants with God? Answering these questions required serious consideration, and I did not take them lightly.

Gratefully, I was morally clean. From the time I had been eight years old, I knew this was a requirement. My whole life I had lived carefully in this matter, knowing I wanted the blessings of the temple for myself and my family. I had dutifully paid my tithing, knowing all I had came from God anyway. Though my parents had not always observed the Word of Wisdom, the sweet whisperings of the Spirit had confirmed in my soul the importance of my obedience to this law. My experience in Washington, D.C., had been but one example. I would understand later why this law played such a significant role in my life. I also loved God. For my whole life, He had been my comfort. In many ways, I believe He raised me. And I looked forward to making promises to Him that I was willing to keep throughout my life, knowing that in return, I would be bound to Him and my family forever.

I was taught this process of being sealed to Kent would take several steps. First, I would be prepared through ceremonial initiatory ordinances. Following this, I would then receive my endowment. I was reminded the word *endowment* meant gift—in this case the gift of understanding how to obtain eternal life.

This would be my opportunity to make covenants with God. In the Old Testament again, Moses led Israel to camp before Mount Sinai where God told Moses, "If ye will obey my voice indeed, and keep my covenant, then ye shall be a peculiar treasure unto me above all people: for all the earth is mine: and ye shall be unto me a kingdom of priests, and an holy nation" (Exodus 19:5-6). When Moses returned with this direction to the people, they responded, "All that the Lord hath spoken we will do" (Exodus 19:8). My endowment would give me the opportunity to declare likewise.

Since Kent had served a mission, he had already received his own endowment. I received mine two days before our actual sealing. I understood that on the day of our sealing, we would be taken to a sealing room where a priesthood holder who had been given these "keys of the kingdom" would seal us "for time and all eternity." Kent and I would kneel across from each other at an altar and be bound as one forever. I looked forward to hearing the words. When I had been sealed to my mother and father by proxy, I was not there to hear them be sealed. They brought us children in the room after this ordinance had taken place. Much of my anticipation rested on this point.

Maybe it was because I had attended many weddings outside the temple. Though the ceremonies were unique and conducted differently, they always ended with the words, "Till death do you part." I hated that. I'm sure that losing my father so early in life made me sensitive. I had lived through the finality of "Till death do you part," and it came much sooner than expected. But our marriage would be different. After we had been sealed, I would never "lose" Kent. He would be mine forever, and any children we had would be ours as well. I loved him. I couldn't wait to hear the words.

Kent had a microbiology final on the day I was to receive my endowment. We were both incredibly stressed finishing up classes, finding a place to live, and making preparations for our wedding. I can safely say we were a little short with each other. As hard as I tried to stay calm, I became more irritated as the day went on. By the time Kent arrived to take me to the temple in the afternoon, I could hardly function. Every movement took such effort. Kent recognized immediately what was happening. He gave me a big hug. "This happens to people before they get baptized, too. We are spiritual beings and subject to spiritual forces. There is opposition in all things, especially when you are taking such an important step as making temple covenants."

The moment Kent said those words, I felt the opposition pull harder. But as I recognized it as the source of my fatigue and frustration, it immediately left.

Kent smiled and said, "It seems like every time I go to the temple, something comes up to make it more difficult."

I have thought about this experience since and recognized it as the beginning of my own spiritual training. The feeling I had was not one of, *You are making a mistake. Don't go through with this.* It was more oppressive, as though I were swimming through sand. The experience confirmed Kent's words. I was a spiritual being and subject to spiritual forces.

I arrived at the temple with an understanding of what would take place, not knowing exactly how it would happen. It took no more than fifteen minutes to receive my initiatory ordinances. This ceremonial washing and anointing was personal and powerful. Every word opened my soul and enlarged my heart. The beauty of those unspeakable blessings overwhelmed me. God knew me. God loved me. He would help me throughout my life.

So many times in the years that followed, when I would face difficult challenges, I would return to the promises made to me in the washing and anointing and draw courage from that reservoir of hope. I know those blessings have preserved my life and my ability to function on more than one occasion.

The next stage was my endowment. This part took a little longer, about two hours. This was my opportunity to make covenants with God and as the Israelites of old, I committed that, "All that the Lord hath spoken, [I] will do" (Exodus 19:8).

The events of the day changed me forever. I realized I was not just having a spiritual experience. Rather, my whole life I had been a spiritual being having a physical experience. I had a spirit. I knew it because for a few moments and in brief glimpses, I felt God's confirming power and recognized Him. He knew me, and now I knew Him, too.

Two days later, Kent and I were sealed. Our sealer was Elmer Christensen, a friend of Kent's family. While the temple workers prepared the room, Kent and I waited together in the celestial room of the Salt Lake Temple. I couldn't wait to hear the words. What would Elmer Christensen say to seal us and our future family together for eternity? When they led Kent and me into the room, all of our endowed family and friends were gathered there. Before sealing us, Brother Christensen gave us some counsel about marriage, and the one piece of advice that stuck out was, "Let people say those Pearsons do everything together."

Looking back now, after twenty-five years of marriage, Kent and I have to smile. We still intend to take Brother Christensen up on that advice.

Then we knelt on either side of the altar in the middle of the room and were married by the authority of the holy priesthood. I couldn't breathe while Brother Christensen said those marvelous, powerful words that sealed Kent and me together for time and all eternity. I cried as I listened to the wonderful promises, grateful for what they meant to me and this wonderful man I loved. What a relief. We belonged to each other forever.

Following the ceremony, Kent and I stood side by side and looked into the mirrors carefully placed on opposite walls— our reflections repeating endlessly. I could not comprehend the magnitude of forever, or understand how it all worked. I just believed the scripture, "But if ye receive me in the world, then shall ye know me, and shall receive your exaltation; that where I am ye shall be also" (D&C 132:23).

13

THE MISSING PIECE COMPLETES
THE DARK PUZZLE

Kent and I moved into half of a small home located near the Westminster College campus at 1100 East Milton Avenue in Salt Lake City. The wonderful couple we rented from informed us as we settled in, "You will need to take out your own garbage." Since they lived in another house right behind us, we never wanted for anything and considered them our second parents. We also enjoyed the companionship of other newly married couples who over time rented the other side of our same house.

When we married on December 16, 1983, I had one-and-a-half years left to complete my nursing degree, and Kent had two-and-a-half years to go. He was accepted to the Westminster College of Nursing, while I finished my education at the University of Utah.

For my last quarter at the University, I worked alongside a wonderful nurse chosen as my preceptor at St. Mark's Hospital. I also signed a contract to work at that same hospital following my graduation. I remember specifically putting on my form that I did not want to work with cancer patients. The chemotherapy frightened me, and I didn't know if I could cope with the emotional aspects of a potentially terminal illness. This was also a time when we practiced Primary Care Nursing. This meant I had the total care of each of my patients without the use of an aide. I loved this type of care but recognize the health care industry will probably never enjoy that luxury again.

After graduation, I ended up on the Ground Floor with patients suffering from such chronic illnesses as diabetes, kidney failure, various bowel issues, and basically everything that wasn't gynecological, surgical, orthopedic, or related to cancer. Many of my patients were elderly, and I came to love and respect them for their experience and wisdom. My heart was drawn to them. One spry, ninety-year-young woman, who received therapy for a blood clot, told me in vivid detail about life in America at the turn of the nineteenth century.

There were other patients I grew to love. Another woman, a Native-American diabetic patient, returned again and again due to complications with her disease. She eventually lost her feet, her kidneys, and her eyesight. Despite her challenges, she always remained cheerful. I loved caring for her and trying to make her life a little more pleasant. I gave her the care I would have loved to have given my own mother. In return, this woman was more than gracious in her appreciation. She shared with me some of her most sacred experiences. On one occasion, she went into cardiac arrest after surgery. She later described for me some of the marvelous things she experienced during this event. As a result, she told me she was no longer afraid to die. This gave me great comfort when she passed away several months later.

One day while at work, I glanced at one of my co-workers. Her image looked distorted. I closed my left eye, and she looked normal, but when I opened my eye again, I saw her as if through one of those wavy mirrors at an amusement park. *That is weird*, I thought.

When this co-worker asked me what the problem was, I told her, "My left eye is blurry."

She answered, "You should get that checked."

I hesitated. If there was one thing I had observed, nurses were susceptible to suggestion. On my floor, all the nurses kept track of their own fluid intake and output. On the cardiac floor, the nurses constantly checked their pulse rate. When I was occasionally pulled to the oncology floor, the nurses there assessed their lymph nodes. Since I worked with diabetic patients, many of whom had problems with their vision, I didn't want to get too excited. I did, however, make an appointment with an eye doctor who for years had been a friend of our family. His daughter was one of my mother's best friends.

When I saw him, I noticed he put down, "Von Hippel-Lindau Syndrome." He didn't explain the diagnosis, but told me after the examination, "I think you'll be fine. Why don't you come back in six weeks?"

Six weeks later, the vision in the left eye had become even more distorted. His comment was the same, "I think you'll be fine. Why don't you come back in six weeks?"

After six more weeks, I could hardly see out of my left eye. "I think you'll be fine. Why don't you come back in six weeks?"

I looked at him. "I don't think there will be any reason to come back. By then, my vision in that eye will be gone."

I think of that event now, and cannot believe I was so passive. I want to scream at myself, "What were you thinking? You were in nursing! You had all the resources, the physicians, the knowledge; why on earth didn't you do something instead of waiting on this doctor who did nothing?"

I cannot explain my reluctance other than to say he was a family friend. I did not want to offend him. Back then, you trusted that your doctor knew best. Researching something like this required a trip to a University Medical Library and hours looking through catalogues and indexes. Access to the Internet has certainly changed things.

This physician, sensing my emotional frustration, finally gave me a referral to a physician in San Francisco. I immediately made an appointment and arrangements for Kent and me to fly to California.

While boarding the plane, Kent heard a familiar voice. He looked around and asked, "Is that Lana?"

An attractive, dark-haired girl looked up, "Is that you, Kent?"

Lana had dated Kent's younger brother, Steve, in high school. In typical Kent fashion, he said in a way only he could get away with, "Have you had a nose job, Lana? You look great!"

Luckily, she laughed and slapped him. She knew teasing was Kent's sincerest form of endearment. (Actually, Kent is acutely aware of his own rather unique nose. This fact was undoubtedly a joke between the two of them.)

I am grateful I can acknowledge Lana in the story of my life and remember the great kindness she showed us that day. It turned out she lived just thirty minutes from San Francisco. She offered us the use of her apartment and her car. When Kent and I ran into Lana that day, we were newlyweds with our whole lives in front of us. After only a few days, we would leave Lana as completely different people with uncertain futures. She shared this transformation with us.

The next day, we dropped Lana off at work and drove to the physician's office in her car. We sat in the waiting room for seven hours with numerous other patients who had come from all over the world. As I filled out the Family Medical History form, I wrote about my mom and all her brain tumors, Nanny's kidney cancer, and my brother's brain tumor. I secretly harbored a bit of pride at having such an interesting family history.

With a bright headlamp and lens, the doctor scanned my retinas. He looked distinguished with his graying hair and moustache. He stood so close I could smell his expensive cologne. After ten minutes of staring into that searing light with dilated pupils, I heard him say, "Go ahead and sit back." He turned to his desk, sat down, and pushed the 'record' button on his Dictaphone. "The patient has tumors made up of blood vessels in both retinas . . ."

I tried to swallow, but couldn't. Both retinas? Would I lose the vision in my other eye, too? Was I going blind?

He swiveled his chair in my direction, looking at me over his bifocals. "These tumors are called retinal angiomas. Given your family history of brain tumors, I can tell you with 99 percent certainty you have the genetic disease, Von Hippel-Lindau Syndrome (VHL.) It is autosomal dominant, which means men and women are at equal risk; if you have the gene, you will express it, and there is a 50 percent chance you will pass it on to your children."

He handed me a paper filled with terminal possibilities: brain tumors; spinal cord tumors; retinal angiomas; abdominal cysts including the kidney, pancreas, liver, spleen; kidney cancer, and pheochromocytoma–a tumor of the adrenal gland that floods your system with adrenaline, dangerously elevating your blood pressure. Several of the conditions already carried the face of someone I loved.

I stared at the end of my life, written right there on the page.

When Kent and I arrived back at Lana's, I fell into him. "I am so sorry to do this to you."

He held me close. "I already knew. Before we ever got married, I already knew. If I had the choice today, I would still marry you."

I didn't cry just for myself. I cried for Kent and every member of my family. I didn't want to be the one to tell them.

Kent and I had our whole lives planned out. We wanted to have a large family, do service in the community, and be influences in the world for good. Now I couldn't count on any of it. I realized it wasn't my life. It never had been *my* life.

I limped into Lana's small bathroom, closed the door, dropped by the tub, and sobbed a simple prayer, "Heavenly Father, what would You like me to do with my life?"

I suppose this was the moment when I really started living. From that second on, I understood I lived on borrowed time and every day I had was a gift. The remarkable truth is—that's how it had always been, that's how it is for everyone. Not one of us comes into this world with a guarantee. I just didn't see this before.

The doctor treated the tumors in both eyes with laser surgery. The vision in my right eye escaped with little damage to the retina, but on the left, the tumor had grown too large. If I had received treatment sooner, it might have been okay, but as it was, the scar tissue from the laser uprooted the center of my retina, leaving me with double vision. The doctor assured me my brain would compensate and eventually work it out. It took three to four years, but he was right.

When I returned from San Francisco, I broke the news to Mom first. She was sitting in her recliner in the front room of her condo. I said, "These tumors in my eyes, Mom, they're part of a bigger problem. As it turns out, all these brain tumors and problems with your spine are genetic. We have the genetic disease, Von Hippel-Lindau Syndrome."

As I explained the ramifications of the disease for future generations, I couldn't stop the flood of despair.

Mom's voice softened, "Oh, you'll cry for about a week and then you'll get over it."

Her words stopped me. I looked at her, realizing I could be looking at myself. For all my issues with our relationship, Mom had never indulged in self-pity over her own condition. As her body declined, she developed her mind by listening to the classics on tapes supplied by the Blind Center. She took literature classes. Whatever feelings of discouragement and frustration she experienced with her body, she kept them to herself.

I looked at her—a widow trapped in a twisted body she could hardly move now from the shoulders down, her urine draining into a little bag strapped around her leg. What lesson on despair could I teach her? She was right. All those years, I had been utterly ungrateful.

And she was right on another account. It took me about a week to accept my diagnosis and realize that if this was all the life I had, I couldn't waste a single moment feeling sorry for myself.

And as my own emotional noise quieted, heavenly comfort moved in and gave assurance to my soul. God knew. He knew my situation. My life was in His hands. Whatever happened to me, it would be okay.

14

SOMETHING TO TELL

Shortly after my eye treatments were completed in San Francisco, the nursing floor I worked on shut down, and I was moved to another department. I ended up working with the cancer patients. Chemotherapy no longer frightened me. And I no longer worried how I would deal with the emotions associated with a terminal illness. What a rich experience, tailor-made for me at that time of my life.

I admitted one thirty-year-old woman with breast cancer who had an elevated calcium level. The cancer had spread to her bones. It nearly broke my heart to take her medical history. At one point, she touched my wrist, "It's okay. Really, it's okay." I borrowed her courage.

On another occasion, I admitted a woman who had just been diagnosed with leukemia in the doctor's office. She couldn't stop looking in the mirror. "Am I the same person I was this morning? I look exactly the same as I did this morning, and yet, they tell me I'm dying. " Though I didn't pretend to know how she felt, I sympathized with how quickly the entire landscape of our lives can change.

Another patient I loved had been receiving therapy for a blood clot. One morning when I came in, her eyes looked empty.

I sat down on the side of her bed. "What's wrong?" I asked.

"The biopsy showed liver cancer. They tell me I have three months to live."

This one did me in. I didn't even know she was scheduled for a liver biopsy. When I arrived home that afternoon, I wept. It seemed my days were filled with nothing but sorrow. How could there be so much sorrow? My whole body ached.

Toward the end of the evening, something in my body changed. I experienced a searing heat that burned inside of me from head to toe. The power washed through me like waves over and over again. Words came into my mind: "Come unto me, all ye that labour and are heavy laden, and I will give you rest. Take my yoke upon you, and learn of me; for I am meek and lowly in heart: and ye shall find rest unto your souls. For my yoke is easy, and my burden is light" (Matthew 11:28-30). The words lightened me. All of these sorrows belonged to the Savior Jesus Christ. He knew my heart, and these were His burdens to carry. The entire load had been lifted.

I also cared for terminal patients. More than anything in my life, I suppose I had always feared dying the most. I came to recognize death not as a grim reaper, but as a blessed release. I respected the sacred and majestic passage of the spirit from this world to the next. I watched some families in deep conflict over the impending death of their loved one, and others who treated it as an unavoidable event and took the opportunity to resolve all unfinished business. In quiet moments, patients would tell me of visits from those who had already passed on. Messages given were always short, specific, and prophetic. I never took it for granted that I walked those halls with angels.

Of all I learned, this had the most profound impact on me. I didn't fear death, but I was terrified of the process. I asked the nurse practitioner who worked on our floor, "Why does death have to be so painful and agonizing?"

Her answer surprised me. "I don't believe death is any more painful than birth."

I pondered that comment. I had been forced from my mother's womb, separated from all that kept me alive. At the time of my own birth, I bet I thought I was dying. What a wonderful surprise it must have been when I took that first breath.

I came to a new understanding of death and viewed it as a birth into another world. One day, I would simply be born again. When my time came, if I was coherent and aware, I would discuss death openly and offer to take messages to loved ones on the other side.

And speaking of birth, this was also a time of questioning what Kent and I should do about a family. After finding out I had Von Hippel-Lindau Syndrome and that any biological children would have a 50 percent chance of having it, too, I told Kent I couldn't have children. I felt it would be the most selfish decision in the world for me to bear children, knowing I could give them this curse. The patriarchal blessing I had received when I was sixteen told me, "Children will bless your home," but it didn't say how they would come. We decided to adopt.

We met with parents who had adopted. We talked with our bishop and received a referral to the Church's Social Service network. We met with social workers and found out every detail of what our options were and what process we needed to follow.

One of the state's requirements for adoption at that time was a blood test for venereal disease. I remember sitting in the phlebotomist's office watching the tube fill with my blood to see if I had syphilis or gonorrhea. I shook my head. If they were worried about a venereal disease, something that could easily be treated, what would they say about my having VHL?

The social workers gave us a packet to fill out, mostly information about us they could give to a woman wanting to put her child up for adoption. I could not fill out those forms. I tried almost every day, but simply couldn't.

In the meantime, Kent also finished up his nursing program. I couldn't believe they would allow him to graduate when he had never changed a bedpan, but they did. As he hoped, he was quickly hired as a salesperson for Marion Laboratories in Phoenix, Arizona. The company wouldn't allow him to stay in Salt Lake long enough to take his nursing boards. That's how he could graduate from nursing school without being an RN.

I kept thinking, *Maybe that's why I couldn't fill out those forms. It's because we're moving and we will find our baby in Phoenix.*

We moved in 1985 to Ahwatukee, a small community outside of Phoenix. Kent worked for Marion Labs, and I took a job with a durable medical equipment company. This way, I could have normal hours Monday through Friday, without having to work nights or holidays.

I fasted and prayed. Where should we go to find our child? We met with adoption agencies, but after each meeting, I took a gut-check. Was this the place? Nothing. A frustrated, anxious nothing. I became a beggar. "Please tell me what to do? Where are we supposed to go? What am I doing wrong that I can't get an answer?" These questions consumed my thoughts every single day. Perhaps only those who have struggled with the inability to have children will fully understand the agony of those days, weeks, and months.

During this time, I had a powerful spiritual experience. It did nothing to answer the questions about my family, but it did pull me back from this obsession.

I had a sacred dream. In this dream, I was traveling with some dear high school friends with whom I had lost touch. One of them told me she had left the Church. She had prayed to know if the Church was true but didn't receive an answer. I couldn't believe it. This was the friend who had strengthened me during those vulnerable years of high school. She had been my rock. But in my dream, there was a person of great influence present in her life who prevented her from receiving the answers she sought. I began telling her about all the times in my life when God had helped me. While describing these events, I realized they were times when I had not even been aware of God's involvement. As I told each story, I also learned about His intervention on my behalf. I marveled with each incident at all He had done for me.

All of a sudden, the scene changed. I stood in darkness. Little by little my eyes adjusted and I realized I was in the middle of a vast, scorched field. I heard pained moans and could make out shapes of bodies lying all around me on the ground. The air felt heavy and oppressive. *Surely this is the end of the world,* I thought.

A voice answered, "The battle rages for the souls of men." I then realized there was someone who walked with me, though I could not see Him in the darkness.

I noticed shadows of people moving through the field. Two-by-two they knelt by one of the wounded, attending to the injuries, before carrying the body away. "These are the spiritually wounded," I was told.

I realized my friend was somewhere among them.

I woke up, but the power of the dream remained. I thought back over what I had told this friend about the times when God had helped me, but I could not remember the specific events. What a loss. They had been taken from me, but I knew He was in my life far more than I ever imagined. I couldn't sleep. The power of that dream stayed in my room. Several hours later, it was still there. I had to do something.

I went into the kitchen and wrote this friend a letter. "I know you will think I'm crazy. The last time we spoke, you were the Relief Society president in your student ward, but I've had this dream and I can't sleep." I told her about the experience and then finished, "In my dream you said you had prayed, but hadn't received an answer."

When I finished writing the letter, the power from that experience left, and I was able to sleep. Though I'm not sure she ever received it, I did mail the letter. Several weeks later, I ran into a mutual acquaintance who confirmed that my dear friend had indeed left the Church.

Despite my daily unanswered pleas regarding where to find our child, I knew God answered prayers. How I wished I could just see a glimpse of my life in five years time to know how it worked out, or if it worked out. If I just knew, I could stop worrying.

One night, some weeks later, Kent and I had an appointment at the Jewish Community Center to check out yet another adoption agency. The schedule was tight; Kent had a flight to Salt Lake where he had a work meeting and would need to leave right after the appointment. We met with the woman in charge who was very kind. She was encouraging and cheery. So why were my insides in such a knot? Why did I feel as though every nerve in my body wanted to scream?

In the Doctrine and Covenants, it gives guidance for seeking God's help in making important decisions. "Behold, I say unto you, that you must study it out in your mind; then you must ask me if it be right and if it is right I will cause that your bosom shall burn within you; therefore, you shall feel that it is right. But if it be not right you shall have no such feelings, but you shall have a stupor of thought" (D&C 9:9).

After the appointment, I dropped Kent off at the airport. We didn't even get a chance to talk about the meeting. I was glad. My heart still felt itchy and irritated. When I knelt to say my prayers, I could hardly gather my thoughts to begin. Then it hit me. I was confused. Was I having a stupor of thought? I whispered, "Oh. Maybe we aren't supposed to adopt." The anxious feeling in my heart relaxed.

I swallowed and asked, "Am I supposed to have children?" The same power that had been with me the night of my dream returned. It bored straight into my heart until I knew I had received an undeniable answer. I was supposed to have children. My entire body calmed. Even the air in the room became perceptively still and full of peace.

I thought about Kent. We had both agreed we should adopt. Given the ramifications of this decision for our children, I could not make this decision alone. He would need to know for himself. In fact, it was even more important for him to be certain. I swallowed again and asked, "Wilt thou please tell Kent?"

I crawled under the covers, and for the first time since my diagnosis, allowed myself to wonder what it would be like to have a child of my own. I hugged my belly. I could experience giving birth and giving life. I think I bawled for half the night with joy. God had given me a piece of my life back. He had given me permission to have a family. And I trusted Him. Whatever happened, I would trust Him.

Before Kent came home, I kept wondering how to tell him. If I brought it up, I worried he would agree based on my experience, without receiving his own witness. Knowing the reality of my mother's condition and what could happen to our children, he had to know for himself. I prayed for help in knowing what to do.

The day Kent came home, he seemed quiet and tentative. I knew I couldn't bring it up, not with him like this. After a couple of hours of his being unusually solemn, he said, "ML, I need to talk to you." I grimaced, imagining all the worst scenarios of what he might have to say.

He sat me down. "When I went back to Salt Lake, I was so confused. I decided to get a father's blessing from my dad." He looked down and paused for a moment. "In the blessing, ML, he told me you would have most, if not all of our children."

I sighed with relief and gratitude. I nodded my head and smiled. "I have something to tell you, too."

15

YOU SHALL WALK AND NOT BE WEARY

I did not get pregnant right away. Kent and I had been living in Arizona for his job, when another opened up in Salt Lake. In the spring of 1987, we moved back home. Through some family connections, we secured an apartment in the Fort Union area, in the southeast part of the valley. Now I needed to find a job.

In Arizona, I had worked for a durable medical equipment company. It had been a luxury to work regular hours, and I hoped to find something similar. When I found a job listed in the paper for a patient relations representative for the L.D.S. Hospital, I applied. On the day I went in for my interview, Kent sat me down. "You know I'm amazing in interviews, right?"

I nodded, because he actually was. I, on the other hand, hated them, especially the part where they said, "Tell me about your strengths." Maybe it's because of Mom's reactions that I've never been good at bragging.

"Now listen to me," Kent went on, "when you get to the end of the interview, you look the person directly in the eyes and you ask, 'what do I need to do to get this job?' Got that?"

I think he could sense my hesitation. I'm just not that direct.

"Seriously, ML. You have to ask that question."

"Okay," I sighed. As if I didn't have enough to worry about. I really hated interviews.

I interviewed with a man by the name of Richard G. Scott. (He is not the Richard G. Scott known in The Church of Jesus Christ of Latter-day Saints as one of the Quorum of the Twelve Apostles.) This Richard G. Scott was one of the administrators for the L.D.S. Hospital.

As Kent had directed me, at the end of the interview, I looked directly at Mr. Scott and asked, "What do I need to do to get this job?" Maybe I didn't ask it with the same verve Kent expected, but I did ask the question. I don't even remember Mr. Scott's answer, but I did get the job. And he told me later the reason he gave it to me was because I asked that question.

As the patient relations representative for the hospital, I handled all of the patient's complaints. I visited with many of them every day, asking about their hospitalizations and what we could do better. When I think back over my life and determine those experiences that made the biggest difference in who I am, this opportunity to work at L.D.S. Hospital with Dick Scott was one of those.

Dick was one of the most encouraging influences of my life. He was a good man who saw good in others. He taught me that criticism was a gift. How could you make things better if you didn't know there was a problem? This allowed me to be a more sincere listener without taking offense, even with things that were personal. Dick taught me not to argue perceptions. Every person's opinion is valid and important to the person making it. I needed to respect those perceptions and opinions. In many ways, this job refined me. I will forever be grateful to Dick Scott and all he taught me.

I finally did get pregnant, and I felt great. I had waited so long for this child, I didn't register any complaints. As the pregnancy continued, I cherished the feeling of movement. I loved placing my hands on my belly to feel that tiny bundle of life inside. Was that little knob a knee or an elbow? In response to my pressure, whatever it was moved. I watched the video tape of my ultrasound exam over and over again. That shadowy little skeleton was mine and now we knew it was a she and she was alive. Before she was born, we had already given her the name, Janice. According to my sources, this name meant "Gift from God." In so many ways, she was a gift from Him.

There is also something profound about two spirits being encompassed in the same body. I felt the presence of Janice's spirit as an overwhelming sense of love. This confirmed an impression I received that she had the gift of love.

I was about 36 weeks along when I went in for my routine exam. I got to see the doctor every week now. Dr. Quinn put the fetal scope on my abdomen to listen to her heart. We were getting close to being done. We both listened, "Bomp, bomp, bomp, bomp, bomp, bomp, bomp, bomp, bomp, bomp..." The heart was beating, but I could not detect a rhythm. Worried, I looked up at Dr. Quinn.

He looked at me, also worried. "We need to do an ultrasound."

Half a day later, we knew Janice was in heart failure. I was admitted to the hospital and given medications intended for her heart. Although they helped to slow her rate, her rhythm remained abnormal. Subconsciously, my hands encircled my belly, attempting to hold her.

Dr. Quinn assured me, "Once she's born, she'll probably do fine. But until her lungs are mature, she's better off where she is. We'll keep a close eye on things."

I believed him. Once tests showed Janice was ready, I was induced into labor. Janice was born about 3:00 P.M. at the L.D.S. Hospital in February of 1989, and Dr. Quinn was right. In the moments after her birth, her heart began beating normally.

When the nurses finally handed her to me, I could not believe it was Janice. A quick scan of all of her bits and pieces confirmed, she was real. This was actually my child, and after all this time, I was holding her.

A wave of exhaustion flooded over me, and I had no more strength, not even to hold her. Kent scooped her tiny body into his hands and stared into her eyes as if to introduce himself. Subconsciously again, I felt my belly, and for a moment, grieved her absence.

"Welcome to the world," I whispered.

There is something profound about the process of giving birth. To this day, I still have not fully processed the experience, nor do I think I ever will. I gained a new respect and admiration for my body. For nine months, it had single-handedly nourished this child. More importantly, it knew how to do it and did so without conscious effort. I watched as it expanded and made room for her to grow. And now, this body of mine had just delivered my baby. Having had an epidural, I felt only a fraction of its pain.

In those moments while I lay shivering after the delivery, I knew my body was once again reforming and repairing itself. I blinked back my emotion. My body knew how to do so many wonderful things.

I had intended to quit my job at the L.D.S. Hospital after Janice was born. I had a six-week leave of absence, and Dick told me I didn't have to make any permanent decisions until that time was up. Once again, this was benevolence on his part. It would have been easier for him to fill my spot immediately.

Dick was watching out for me. Shortly after Janice was born, Kent's work informed us his contract was being terminated. His employers could not afford our medical insurance, and the company was going in a different direction. Kent and I debated what to do. The new Church President, Ezra Taft Benson, had only recently reminded mothers to make their families their first priority. In situations where possible, mothers were encouraged to stay home and nurture their children.

Given our personal circumstances, Kent and I prayed to know what God wanted us to do. We both received the same answer; I needed to be home with our children. We told the Lord we would make any sacrifice in order to do this and pledged our commitment to the answer He had given us. We also prayed for his intervention on our behalf.

Realizing we could soon be without insurance, we decided I should have all my scans to make sure everything was okay. About a month after Janice's delivery, I was scheduled for an MRI of my brain.

"You need a complete scan of your whole spinal cord," Kent complained.

I knew he was right. I had never actually had an MRI of my spine. At the time, MRIs were still rather new and quite expensive. I called the doctor back.

"I realize you told me I don't need a scan of my spine, but . . ." I explained to him our insurance situation and how all of the current information I was receiving from the VHL Family Alliance demonstrated tumors grew in the spinal cord as well and told him they recommended yearly screenings. "I realize this is something you may see as unnecessary, but for my sake, would you be willing to order the scans of my spine?"

He was.

It was a good thing he did. The MRI of my cervical scan revealed a large tumor that needed to be removed. I was scheduled for surgery the day after we would bless Janice at church. She would be six-weeks old.

Many things weighed heavily on our minds: first of all, the location of the tumor in the cervical spine. Given the reality of my mother's quadriplegia, we knew this was a possibility. Secondly, Kent needed to find a new job. If it had not been for Dick Scott and his encouraging me to take the whole six weeks leave before turning in my notice, I would not have had insurance for my surgery. Beyond that, when I called and told Dick about my tumor, he made arrangements and signed all the paperwork for me to have an additional three months medical leave of absence. Though I would not be paid, I would remain eligible for insurance benefits.

God bless Dick Scott for putting my needs at that time above his own. He knew I would not be coming back; he knew he would not have anyone in that position and many of those responsibilities would fall to him, and he did it anyway. This is but one of many examples of the type of person he is and the dignity and kindness with which he treats everyone. It is a privilege to acknowledge the sweet role he played in my life.

With Dick's help, our burden was lighter, but our lives were still filled with uncertainty on so many fronts. We attended a special service known as stake conference with heavy hearts. Elder Monte J. Brough of the Seventy was the visiting General Authority and seemed to be speaking directly to us. He told of a difficult time in his life and how the promises of keeping the Sabbath day holy manifested themselves through his experiences. They were the exact blessings we needed. We studied the words of Isaiah 58 and section 59 of the Doctrine and Covenants. The blessings that come from keeping the Sabbath day holy were both temporal and spiritual. "And the Lord shall guide thee continually, and satisfy thy soul in drought, and make fat thy bones: and thou shalt be like a watered garden, and like a spring of water, whose waters fail not" (Isaiah 58:11). "Inasmuch as ye [keep the Sabbath day holy], the fulness of the earth is yours" (D&C 59:16).

One night as Kent and I were praying, I had the distinct impression the Lord wanted the very best for us. I looked up at Kent, still bowed in his own personal thoughts. When his head lifted and his eyes opened, I told him, "The Lord wants the very best for us."

Given our present circumstances, it might have seemed a mockery, except for the powerful feeling in our hearts that assured us, He truly cared. He would be with us, and He would see us through.

While I waited for my surgery, I had my own private conversations with God. Knowing He wanted the best for us, I told Him I trusted Him. If my being a quadriplegic was the best for us, I trusted Him. But I did tell Him I had to know if that would be the case. I had to know when I held Janice for that last time before my surgery, if that would be the last time I would ever be able to hold her again. I had to know. I never mentioned this need to know beforehand to Kent.

I considered every moment with Janice a gift. It was such a pleasure to care for her. On the day of her blessing, early in April of 1989, I celebrated her life with bittersweet feelings. My desire to know the outcome of my surgery before I went in the next morning had not been answered. Later that evening, after all the family and friends had said their good-byes, Kent and his father paused to give me a blessing. Ralph placed a drop of consecrated oil on my head. He then placed his hands on my head, addressed me by name and declared that through the power of his Melchizedek Priesthood, he was anointing me with oil consecrated for blessing the sick and the afflicted. He did this in the name of Jesus Christ. Kent then placed his hands upon my head to seal the anointing. Immediately after addressing me by name, and declaring his authority as a holder of the Melchizedek Priesthood also, he said these words, "You shall run and not be weary, you shall walk and not faint." I did not hear the rest of the blessing. My mind and heart rested in the comfort of those words.

I recognized them immediately. They were the promises given to those who obey the Word of Wisdom found in Section 89 of the Doctrine and Covenants. This is the health law outlining, among other things, abstinence from coffee, tea, and alcohol. Under every circumstance, I had been careful to live this law. From a very early age, the Spirit had impressed on me its importance. Now I understood why. The Lord knew I would need those blessings.

I wish I could tell you that when I held Janice for that last time before leaving for the hospital, I had no worries. I held her in my hands, memorizing the feel of her weight. I rubbed her cheeks with my thumbs, memorizing the feel of her skin, and lifted her to my chest, inhaling the smell of her newness. I relished the sound of her breathing in my ear. Just in case, I wanted to remember everything of how she felt. As I handed her back to Kent's mother so we could go, I placed my own life in God's hands, hoping and praying He would keep His promise to me.

And through the skilled hands of my dear neurosurgeon, He did. I woke from the surgery to the feel of a blood pressure cuff on my arm and the weight of the covers on top of my legs. I took in a deep breath and opened my eyes. How wonderful it was to feel.

"Can you move your toes," the nurse asked.

I could. I felt them rub against the sheets.

"Can you squeeze my fingers?" I felt her warm fingers slip inside my palm. I could hug them with my hand.

Later that night, the nurses helped me so I could sit up in bed. And the next day, I could walk.

When Kent's mom brought Janice up, I couldn't hold her on my own because of her weight, but I could feel her. I had no doubt that after my recovery, I would be able to meet and care for her needs. The only complications I experienced in my recovery were actually related to postpartum changes and those were manageable.

And Kent did get a job. He was hired by Critikon, a division of Johnson and Johnson. We had excellent medical insurance without a preexisting condition clause. We certainly were not wealthy, but I can honestly say every one of our needs was met. We had this beautiful new member of our family. And we fully realized where our blessings came from. I'm glad I did not know then how much more God would teach us.

16

THE LICORICE LESSON

I loved being a mother, but for the first few weeks after the surgery on my spine, I could not hold Janice. I will forever be grateful to Kent's mother for taking care of me in those first two weeks. Because she worked full time, Kent's sisters took turns coming over during the day to care for me and Janice. We lived with Nanny for the third week after my surgery. She bathed Janice with a natural, caressing rhythm, and spoke to her in a language Janice understood. Her eyes widened, and her tiny chin lifted to taste Nanny's words. The two of them bonded instantly. What a privilege for me to observe all these mothers, mothering my child.

This experience also gave me a new perspective of God as a parent. I never realized before how much He could love me until I had my own child. I felt I understood Him better now.

Memories of my own mother during this time are strangely absent. I have no recollection of phone calls or relayed messages of concern. Nothing. Just a leftover residue of resentment over how much time I spent with the "Pearsons." I cannot imagine what she must have been going through or how she felt about being unable to help or participate in the birth of my child or my surgery. I will never know. She never made any comment or reference afterward, at least not one that I can remember.

I suppose it was a fair criticism that we spent a lot of time with the Pearsons, but Kent's family did so much for us. His mother and father stepped in whenever there was a need. Before we even thought of what to do about dinner on a difficult day, food was at the door. They spoiled me with affection and kindness. Their anticipation of our every need brought sweetness to a bitter time.

Despite all this mothering early in her life, Janice was not particularly cuddly. "If I must," seemed to be her attitude. She could only handle being held close for so long, and then she had to be off, taking care of important business such as emptying a drawer or exploring a book shelf.

When Janice was about eight-months old, we were on our way out to Bountiful to visit Mom. Janice was strapped into her carrier in the backseat and not acting fussy. She loved car rides and usually never made a sound. On a whim, I decided to let her try a piece of licorice. I had an opened bag sitting next to me, and since she had been introduced to lots of new foods already, I thought she might enjoy a piece of licorice.

I took a single red twist and handed it to her in her car seat. A few seconds later, I heard sucking noises. I looked in the rearview mirror to see her tiny legs kicking with wild enthusiasm. She loved it. Each time I looked back, red licorice slobber had dripped thicker and further, and her eyes were filled with wonder.

After a bit of time, I noticed the piece of licorice had become alarmingly skinny and small. She still had it gripped tightly in her fist and seemed to be enjoying it even more than before. Realizing she could choke on what was left, I reached back and took it from her hand.

She let out a heart-shuddering scream. I don't know why I was surprised, other than she had never screamed with this sense of emergency before. She shrieked with such intensity, she stopped breathing.

I pulled the car over onto the shoulder of the freeway and flew over the backseat. It took several more seconds in my arms before she began wailing again. Now we were both covered in licorice juice. Though she was still crying, I strapped her back into her seat and continued on, not wanting to be stopped on the freeway. It's a good thing I didn't wait. She cried passionately for at least another hour after I reached Mom's and took her inside.

As I paced with Janice in my arms, trying to calm her, I regretted ever giving her the licorice. She was unhappier now than if she had never tried it. What a sad affair. Were there things I shouldn't give her, knowing they wouldn't last forever, and she would be angrier when they were gone?

The thought stunned me. I was no different in that way than Janice. My skin prickled and I took in a sharp breath. Were there things God could not give me, knowing they wouldn't last forever, and that I would be angrier when they were gone? Were there things He knew would make me unhappier for having had them? "How sad," I whispered.

I pondered this thought for quite some time before making a decision. I promised God that if ever He had to take something away from me—and I wasn't just talking about things on my list, I included capabilities such as my eyesight or my ability to walk. I promised Him I would not be angry. Instead, I would be grateful He had ever seen fit to give it to me in the first place. I would be thankful for the time I had been given to enjoy such a gift.

In making this promise, I thought I had put everything of worth to me on the platter. Years later, I would learn I had not considered everything. He would put this promise to the ultimate test.

A few months after this experience with the licorice, Mom's day-help left. When Rob married Anita, and moved out, it left another bedroom open in Mom's condo. Since her needs had become more demanding, we had a woman for the day, who slept downstairs, and another helper for the night, who lived in my old room next to Mom's.

Kent and I talked. Since Mom could no longer walk or support her weight with her legs, it was difficult to find women with the strength to lift her. The day person had to dress Mom in bed then transfer her to a wheelchair. The caregiver then had to transfer her again into a recliner in the living room. There was additional lifting on days when she needed a bath. These were done, however, at a time convenient for both the day and night person so the lifting could be done by two people. Though Mom couldn't have weighed more than 70 pounds, her inflexible, contorted body made lifting her awkward.

We decided I would take care of Mom during the day. I wouldn't sleep there but would commute every morning with Janice and spend the day until the night person took over. Kent insisted I be paid the wages of the day person. We certainly weren't desperate for the two hundred dollars (part of the wages included room and board,) but Kent did not want to start a pattern. This was a vestige of watching his parents make all the sacrifices for his grandmother, without any participation from other family members. Rob and Sue had no argument.

I was happy to take care of Mom, glad to have the experience and expertise now of my nursing degree. I also thought this would be an opportunity for her to interact with her grandchild.

I suppose I was hoping for some positive feedback. After all, I'd made my career caring for the sick. When I touched her, I tried to add an extra measure of tenderness. I did my best to keep her condo clean and attractive. Though I wasn't a great cook, I asked for Mom's input and tried new recipes she suggested. I thought Janice would provide some interest and entertainment other than Mom's usual sixteen hours of television. On some occasions, I must have grown so desperate for a positive comment I would say something such as, "I don't even clean like this at home."

Here's the thing though, everyday my heart filled with compassion for Mom. I was a witness to the ravages inflicted on her body. As I dressed her each morning, I marveled at her condition. Her body had become a study of skeletal anatomy, displaying every bony prominence, muscle, and tendon.

Her years of immobility and random spasms left her joints frozen in contraction. I tried doing range of motion exercises with her, but despite their being painful, on a body that could not feel, they also triggered more muscle spasms. When this happened, it was as though her body was possessed as her muscles ruthlessly contorted her joints even tighter. It took all my strength to separate her tiny knees from her chest in order to short circuit the clenched muscles, leaving us both breathing heavily and dripping with sweat. I am sure Mom could see this general tightening and curling of her frame. Her feet had permanently dropped and twisted on themselves. I could only fit them into shoes using custom made braces that hugged her lower limbs from her toes to her knees. I would love to have known what Mom thought or how she coped with such change.

More shocking than her body's appearance was the lack of function. An indwelling urinary catheter drained into a bag clipped to the side of her bed. Her fingers startled me the most. Normally, hands maneuver, and each finger is capable of incredible, independent manipulation. With Mom, I had to position her hands. When I slipped on her sleeve, each finger had to be accounted for, along with her thumb. Whenever I adjusted or touched those fingers, I shuddered at their coldness and inability to convey or receive tenderness or affection.

I knew I would never please my mom, but it didn't stop me from trying. Despite my efforts to make the time I spent with her pleasant, there was not an easy feeling between us. She lived in a body without function or feeling, and I often wondered if she had banished all emotions as well. I learned not to say anything of a personal nature about me, Kent, Janice, or anything outside of my day with her. The less I included her in my life, the better we got along. I did not tell her when I found out I was pregnant again. The doctor told me I could still lift Mom as long as there wasn't a problem with my pregnancy.

When we lived in our old house on Vista View Drive in Salt Lake City, Mom had some wonderful visiting teachers, Virginia and Suzanne. Mom had a great deal of respect for them, knowing they were dignified women and wives of prominent physicians. Mom had known Suzanne from college. They were also women of integrity and though Mom was not interested in religion, she was deeply moral.

When Mom moved to Bountiful, these two friends packed up our entire house without one word of complaint to me about my not being any help, which I wasn't. These dear women still visited with Mom in Bountiful on a weekly basis. I noticed one thing during this time with my mother. In the beginning, she wasn't any happier with God than she was with me. But as these sincere and caring women visited with Mom every week, I noticed a softening on her part toward God.

On one occasion, one of her old childhood friends dropped by for a visit. He had grown up with Mom and knew her as a vigorous, active person. They reminisced about how Mom was such a tomboy and the first one out on the basketball court every day. She was an asset to any impromptu team, and though a girl, was usually one of the first to be chosen. She could do anything better than the boys. She beat my father at tennis regularly. When he finally defeated her in a match, he refused to ever play her again. On a trip to Cypress Gardens in Florida, it only took one waterskiing ride for them to offer her a job. At the University of Utah, she was recruited for the ski team. It might not have been such a big deal, but they didn't even have a women's team. She competed against men.

I had so few memories of Mom even walking without assistance. After her old friend left, I couldn't help but say, "Oh, Mom, of all the people in the world to go through this, I am so sorry it is you. For someone who had such an appreciation for her body and what it could do and who took so much enjoyment out of life from its function, I am so sorry."

In a rare glimpse of her inner landscape she told me, "If I can go through this, so you don't have to, I am happy to do it."

I stared at her body as my hand clenched the collar of my shirt. She was suffering for me. I tucked those words deep in my heart, right in the hole that for my whole life had been so vacant. Now I understood why she never complained about her condition or used it as an excuse.

Though my mother was not a religious person, she taught me more about the Atonement than I had learned in a lifetime of study. From that moment on, whenever I imagine the Savior, Jesus Christ, atoning for the sins of the world, I hear Him say, "If I can go through this, so you don't have to, I am happy to do it."

17

A PART OF ME

One day while taking care of Mom, I began spotting. Since I was pregnant, I became concerned I might be losing the baby. Fortunately, after several days, the bleeding stopped, but the experience reminded me that at some point in the next few months, I would not be able to lift mom. Given the difficulty of finding good help, it was probably best to start looking.

I told Mom, "We need to find someone new to take care of you during the day."

She asked, "Why's that?"

Without any emotion or expectation I answered, "I'm pregnant."

We didn't discuss it any further other than to talk about what we needed to do to find her new help.

During this time, Virginia and Suzanne, Mom's visiting teachers, started reading scriptures with Mom, something I could never have done. Mom began asking questions. She started thinking about what they talked about and it changed her. When we found another woman able and willing to take over the days, Mom was a little softer.

My pregnancy continued without a problem. When we went for the ultrasound, the fetus was situated in such a way the technician could not determine the sex. It didn't matter. Kent knew it was a boy. Whenever anyone asked, he always answered, "It's a boy." I chuckled, not having the same absolute conviction.

By this time, Janice was mobile. Incredibly mobile. Exhaustingly mobile. The day we brought our new little boy home from the hospital, Janice fell off the counter at Kent's mom's and dad's house and broke her foot. While waiting for the assistant to put on the cast I asked him, "Could you put some lead in that thing to slow her down?"

He smiled and shook his head. "It would only make her stronger and quicker in the end."

What a profound truth.

I wish I had more memories of my deliveries or how it felt to hold my babies for the first time. With Janice, I was so exhausted I could hardly manage her weight. When they handed me our "Little Boy Pearson," I took one look and thought, "This is Janice." The two of them looked so similar. We couldn't decide on a name. For two weeks he was known as "Little Boy Pearson" until Kent and I finally agreed on Andrew.

Before I had children, I didn't understand love. I didn't understand grace. But following their births, the connection was immediate. I would have given my life for these little ones. This was an area of tremendous concern for me before they arrived. I wondered if I would feel about caring for them the same way I felt about caring for Mom. What a relief to discover no resentment as I served their needs. Getting up with them in the middle of the night, though tiring, was a thrilling excuse to look on those tiny little faces. I was so blessed.

One night while resting on the couch, after Janice and the baby had gone to bed, I noticed a big lump just under my rib cage. Medical tests uncovered numerous and large cysts in my pancreas. But that wasn't the biggest concern. I also had cysts in both kidneys and one had a solid tumor. A painful biopsy confirmed it was in fact kidney cancer. I wasn't too surprised. It had been foretold.

The surgery involved two specialties. Dr. Stevens (Virginia's husband and a general surgeon) performed a rewiring of my bowel to reduce the pancreatic cysts, and Dr. Sorenson, a urologist, removed the tumor, as well as all the cysts situated in both kidneys. Fortunately, he was able to preserve most of the kidney function.

Another postpartum surgery. My body still oozed and ached from giving birth, but there I was with one more scar like an upside down smile, following the line of ribs on my belly.

Kent took one look and said, "I think I should start calling you 'Slash'."

"I guess this is one way to lose baby weight."

The surgery had removed a portion of my small intestine, and I couldn't eat for about ten days. After three weeks, I weighed less than I did when I got married. (I'm not complaining about that part.) But I am still amazed at how my body responded. It was alive, could create and nurture a baby from one cell to eight pounds in nine months, and when the process was over, had its own mechanism for giving birth before starting the process to return everything to normal. Now add surgery to that, cutting into organs, removing tissue, suturing it all together, and voila, the body healed on its own. Absolutely incredible.

✗ But as amazing as my body was at doing all of that, my body was also creating those lovely tumors. I was creating my own trauma. Scans had picked up a new brain tumor as well. How could I reconcile that this disease was a part of me and a part of who I was? This dysfunction was encoded into my instructions for living.

✗ I spent a great deal of time considering what I was doing to myself. I had now lost most of the vision in my left eye, undergone the removal of a spinal cord tumor, lost part of my bowel and kidneys, and had the possibility of a brain surgery looming. Was this disease defining me? Was I my disease, or did

I still have a choice? I had two children to raise while living with this disease every day for the rest of my life.

✕ Through prayer, I made some very important decisions. First of all, I could choose the focus of my life. I was not my disease. I was a wife, a mother, a daughter, and a friend. I would schedule my follow-ups and attend my regular doctor's appointments. If necessary, I would have surgery, but other than that, I would not let it occupy my thoughts. I would not waste time or give it energy by talking about it, fearing it, or living my life around it. I explained to Kent that I didn't want other people to define me by my illness either. When I went through surgeries or had difficulties, I didn't want it advertised. The fewer people it affected, the better. I cringed at being known as "that woman with all the tumors."

This proved harder than I imagined. The members of my ward were so caring and thoughtful. They considered it a privilege to help anyone in need. I know many of their feelings were hurt, thinking I didn't consider them close enough or important enough to be included in my distress. That was certainly not the case.

I tried explaining to them once the trap of sympathy. It has a subtle, yet powerful affect and the need for sympathy can actually become addictive. I saw this as a nurse in the hospital. I would never have believed that people could wish themselves ill for sympathy, if I had not seen it for myself. Some people gave up their lives, their ability to enjoy true relationships, and their joy, all for sympathy. They chose to be defined by their illness. They became their disease.

Mom taught me this. Years before, she had some visitors. They told her how sorry and how tragic it was for her to lose her husband at such a young age, and how terrible it was that she had suffered so much. They continued about how hard it must be to raise children not being able to walk. They went on and on about all she had been through. When they left I said, "Wasn't that sweet of them to stop by and say such nice things."

There was Mom, confined in a twisted body to a chair. All Mom could move was her head. She looked at me and rolled her eyes before saying, "Sympathy is a small reward for this."

Rather than be pitied, I wanted to overcome my challenges with dignity and courage. I didn't want to focus on the sorrow, the injustice, or the pain. I intended to use each event as an opportunity to be more submissive to the will of God with gratitude.

Once again, Kent agreed. In keeping with my wishes, he didn't offer his sympathy. Questions such as, "What can I do for you?" or "How are you feeling?" were replaced with statements such as, "I need you to get better."

Before my surgery, our bishop had stopped by and offered to have the ward fast and pray for me. I so appreciated this kind gesture. There I was, a young mother with a new little baby, and a diagnosis of kidney cancer. I would be lying if I said I wasn't afraid. Here he was offering the faith and prayer of so many good people on my behalf. But I trusted God. He had always known best. I knew He would do whatever was right for me and my loved ones. I knew it, even if the outcome was not what we wanted. Some people go through tragic events or episodes, but that's what it is, a one-time request. I would be living with this my whole life, one new tumor to follow yet another. "Thank you, Bishop," I told him, "but that won't be necessary."

In my case, God was once again merciful. The cancer was encased inside the tumor and no other treatment was required. I received the necessary help from Kent, his family and close friends, and I returned to being a mother.

With this new little boy, I felt a kindred spirit. He suffered from colic and cried for his first four months of life. Someone mentioned it might just be his personality to be cranky. Just as Kent knew he would be a boy from the very beginning, I knew Andrew was not cranky. He was my best snuggler, and he loved to rock and cuddle. His hair came in more blonde every day. One early morning as he gestured for me to pick him up out of his crib, I recognized him as the little boy in my dream when I was a teenager. I thought back to the dream and could now identify the facial features, hair color, and the reaching. What touched me most was the memory of how much I loved that child and how his need filled me, the exact sense of what I was feeling at that very moment.

Because of my surgery, we did not bless Andrew in church until he was over four-months old. And he was a huge baby. At three months, he weighed eighteen pounds. After his blessing, one of our good friends teased, "That's the first baby we've ever blessed who had facial hair."

I believe it was at Andrew's baby blessing that Nanny took me aside, looked into my eyes, and shook her finger. "You shouldn't have any more children."

I braced myself. This was my grandmother, a woman I loved and respected. She had not merely expressed her opinion but had given me a directive. I nodded, not so much in agreement, but in acknowledgement of what I must have represented. She, herself, had one kidney removed for kidney cancer, her daughter was quadriplegic and physically devastated from this disease, and here I was, a granddaughter having just recovered from kidney cancer after giving birth to her great-grandchild. I was her unfortunate legacy, possibly passing on her defect.

18

TANGLED UP IN KNOTS

One summer the bishop asked Kent and me to attend Youth Conference with the Young Men and Young Women of our ward. We participated with the youth in negotiating a ropes course, and one of the challenges was called the "Lifeline."

The bishop blindfolded each person then took them one by one to a cord. His verbal instructions were, "Follow this cord to the end."

This should have been easy, but I kept getting caught up in the knots. The cord started out straight, but before long, it became knotted with different cords leading in different directions. Rather than moving forward, I wanted to follow the bishop's instructions exactly. I meticulously followed the cord with my fingers over and under and around the knot, frustrated when the cord wound back on itself and the knot became increasingly more complex, leading me into more and more knots. It took me forever to reach the end of the Lifeline. When the bishop took off my blindfold, he looked perplexed. I had taken longer to get through than anyone—than all the people in our group combined. I had made the task more difficult and harder than it should have been. I will process this self-revelation for the rest of my life.

This experience happened at a crucial time in my life as Kent and I once again debated whether or not I should go back to work after Andrew was born. Several concerns weighed in on this decision.

I had so few memories of my mother mothering me. These sparse memories were similar to damaged, old photographs, and I had only three or four. One was when she came to pick us up from the Salt Lake Swimming and Tennis Club after swimming lessons. In the searing heat, she hadn't worn shoes and had walked on the black asphalt in her bare feet to herd us back to the car. By the time we arrived home, her feet were blistered with second-degree burns. She didn't know. She couldn't feel her feet.

The second was watching her cook the only meal I ever remember her making. She stirred a white sauce, ready to put in the limp, packaged meat and peas before spooning the mixture over toast. I was perched on a chair watching her stir the pan. I don't know why I kept this memory over so many more important ones. I didn't even like Chipped Beef on Toast.

The third was before she was ill and took me skiing on Big Mountain, a ski resort that was once at the top of Emigration Canyon. Mom was pulling me up to sit beside her on the moving chair lift, but I was too small. As the chair rose, I wasn't tall enough to reach the seat and was hanging on by my elbows. I could only hang on for so long before I dropped from the chair into the snow that seemed so far below.

The fourth was after I had been hit by a car as a toddler. I sat in Grandad's medical office at the clinic as he held my arm, checking it over. Mom sat beside me.

Strangely, there is so little movement or life in these memories—just snapshots of the events where the people aren't even breathing.

As I considered being a mother, and whether or not I should stay home with my new baby, this lack of memories haunted me. I wanted my children to have hundreds of thousands to choose from. I wanted to take a leading role throughout their lives.

The other issue affecting my decision was my appreciation for the importance of modeling. When Kent and I got married, there were so many things I did not know how to do. For example, I had never seen anyone clean out a fridge or wipe down a baseboard. As I stumbled along trying to perform some of these unfamiliar duties, Kent would often give me this "did you grow up on the moon" stare and wouldn't even have to say anything. He knew I had (grown up on the moon). To this day, I still do not have curtains. I have no idea how to take care of them. So I wanted my children to see me answering the phone, putting away the laundry, and cleaning out a tub. I wanted them to learn how to do the everyday things most people take for granted.

Kent agreed. We decided that whatever the sacrifice, I would stay home to raise our children. We did not know I would need surgery on my spinal cord after Janice's delivery. Luckily, since my leave of absence was still in effect, most of the cost of the surgery was covered by my insurance. Even then, our portion of the bill was substantial.

When I stopped taking care of Mom because I was pregnant with Andrew, we could not find help willing to do the work for $200.00 a month plus room and board. While the expenses for her day and night help increased, Mom ran out of money.

We had Andrew, followed by my abdominal surgery. Though we had good insurance, our portion, again, was another substantial sum.

During this time, Kent's net income for the month was roughly $1,400.00, $700.00 of which we spent on Mom and her care. Rob and Sue both paid an equal amount.

When Kent and I met with the bishop for tithing settlement, I looked at our budget assessment and wanted to cry. (Each family meets once a year with the bishop to declare whether or not they are full tithe payers. At that time, a budget assessment was also given each family to cover the costs of ward activities. This has since changed and budget assessments are no longer requested.) Our budget assessment that year was the same as when I had been working and Mom could meet her own expenses. Our assessment for the year above and beyond our tithing was $440.00. I remember Kent telling the bishop, "We'll pay it."

Truly, we were not destitute. We did have a reserve. A small trust had been set up for me after my father died. It had been poorly managed, and I had used some of this to support Mom before she sold her home and moved to Bountiful. My paternal grandparents had also passed away and since my father was also deceased, their inheritance came directly to us children. Realizing, however, that I was on track for having surgery every other year, Kent and I knew it wouldn't be long before the money would be gone.

Once again, Kent and I decided we needed to keep the Sabbath day more holy. We sacrificed our "wants," paid our budget assessment, and prayed for help.

Adding another layer of difficulty, after Andrew came and I had been through my kidney surgery, my nursing license came up for renewal. I didn't have the necessary hours. Given all of these circumstances, we decided I should work two Saturdays a month so I could keep my license. Kent could be with the kids while I worked.

Kent interviewed for a new job. He desperately wanted to get on with GE. They had just come out with an updated Magnetic Resonance Imager (MRI.) The University of Utah had just purchased one and Kent figured every hospital would eventually want to have one as well. He was right about that, but after six intense interviews, and his using up almost all of his vacation days flying to one city or another at our own expense, they did not offer him the job. We couldn't figure it out. With his nursing degree, he was the most qualified, and he also had the most sales experience.

Our situation at the time felt so oppressive. Mom wasn't getting any better and her expenses were rising. We were in a two-bedroom apartment where Janice and Andrew shared a room with no hope of ever moving into anything bigger. And now Kent had been denied his coveted job with GE.

I often reflected on that impression I had after Janice was born that "God wanted the best for us." How could I reconcile this with our lives? As I was thinking about it one day, I remembered having that frustrating feeling before—when I had been in the middle of the ropes course and so tangled up in all those knots. The thought finally occurred to me back then—I must be doing something wrong. Blindfolded, I had slowly backed myself out of all the confusing knots until the cord became simple again. This time, when I moved forward and just let the knots slip through my hand, instead of trying to follow every twist and turn with my fingers, I was able to follow the cord in the right direction.

When I felt God tell me He wanted the best for us, it was as though He had backed me out of the knots. I was curious to see how He would bring it to pass.

The next week, a head hunter called Kent to set up an appointment with a company called Advanced Cardiovascular Systems, ACS. They sold cardiovascular balloons and devices used in interventional cardiology.

The day Kent got that job, our lives changed. They also had excellent insurance and would cover all of us with our preexisting conditions. Since the pay was based on commission, if Kent did well, it would be possible for us to someday buy a home. The only drawback with this job was Kent would have to travel. His territory included Colorado, Utah, and Montana. I worked the necessary hours to renew my nursing license and then quit to be home full time with my family.

I look back, and Kent has been doing this same job for over fifteen years. His territory has changed here and there, but he has been part of a technological miracle. In the early days of his career, cardiologists were limited and many patients ended up having bypass surgery where a surgeon opened up the chest, took vessels from the legs, and surgically grafted them onto the heart. The recovery was brutal, and the replaced veins only had about a ten-year lifespan before the surgery would need to be repeated. Hospital stays were long with potential for life-threatening complications and enormous medical expenses.

Over the past fifteen years, Kent has been part of a huge transition to less invasive cardiac procedures. People don't usually have bypass surgery anymore. The technology and techniques have become so specialized, a patient with a heart blockage can have an angioplasty in the morning and go home that same day without an incision. And they generally feel better than they have in a long time.

If Kent had been given that job at GE, he would have taken it. He shudders about that now. It would have been a mistake. The blindfold is gone. The job he ended up with was a much better fit.

On another front, this process of not getting what we wanted, but in the end receiving something better was again repeated. When we began looking for a home, one in our neighborhood became available. I loved that home. We knew and adored the family who owned it. They had added a beautiful addition and the backyard was large and professionally landscaped. We made an offer we could afford, but they couldn't accept. I was heartbroken, but we bought a lot and hoped to eventually build a home. In the meantime, another home in our neighborhood became available. This "happened" to be a bank foreclosure, with larger bedrooms and more usable space on the main level than the first home I loved. The entry into this home was also much easier, a factor that would be of great importance later on. We ended up buying this home. Within weeks, the real estate market went berserk. If we had waited, we would have missed the opportunity.

Our home, which I have come to love, is in a quiet little cul-de-sac, nestled in between two of the most nurturing women I have ever known. Helen lives behind me and Edie lives next door. And a wonderful new family moved into the other home I loved. Diane S. has become one of my idols and a dear friend.

Not long after we moved into our home, Mom's day help informed us she was leaving. The job had become too physically demanding for her to continue. I dreaded having to find someone new. Mom had bedsores now that required complicated care and dressings. The level of her disability had crept up her spine, affecting the muscles that helped her breathe and cough. Who would be able to handle this? In my heart, I knew the time had come to bring Mom into our home, especially now the way had been opened for us to have a home. But I couldn't bring this up to Kent.

While Kent and I were dating, my mother was a source of disagreement. I once told Kent whomever I married would need to consider that my mother might live with us at some point. At the time, he calmly responded, "Well, then maybe now is a good time for us to stop dating. I have no intention of ever living with my mother-in-law." He had lived his entire life with his grandmother and had seen the difficulty it created for his own father. If we ever married, having my mother live with us would never be an option.

I asked God to intervene. I told Him, "You've given us a home, and I believe my mother needs us to care for her here. If that's right, Kent needs to be the one to suggest it."

After a week of my unsuccessful attempts to find someone, anyone, to care for Mom, Kent came to me and said, "I think maybe we should talk about having your mom live with us."

By this time, Sue and her husband, Russ, had moved back to the Salt Lake area, and they felt the same as we did about providing a place for Mom in our homes. They lived in Riverton about seven miles away from our new house. We sat down and worked out a plan. Mom would live with Sue for two months then come and live with me for two. Since Rob and Anita lived in Michigan, they would pay a specified amount to the person caring for Mom that month in order to offset the additional costs. We assured Mom we would not sell her condo until we all felt comfortable with the situation. Since Sue and I both had young children, we made arrangements for home health care to get Mom up in the mornings and put her to bed at night. They would also bathe her twice a week and treat her wounds.

Sue and I could never have done it without these caring women. They became some of Mom's closest friends and her connection to the outside world. The larger bedrooms, extra space on the main level, and easy entry into our home became necessary blessings.

When I brought Mom in for the first time, I had the most profound impression. I wheeled her into her room and felt I had walked through another dimension. I was taking care of myself. Everything I did for her, I was really doing it for me. This impression went above and beyond the Golden Rule. We shared this same disease. Perhaps in my future, I would be in her same situation. In caring for her, I was caring for me. This feeling never left for the entire time she was with us.

I mentioned the amazing medical advances made during this time. Research had also uncovered some interesting facts about our disease, VHL. We were missing a tumor suppressor gene. Rather than stopping the growth, our bodies assisted the tumor. I should not have been surprised when I saw pictures of what the tumors looked like. They were lumps of tissue, covered in blood vessels, tangled like knots.

Given that we had help both night and morning, on the surface it would seem an easy thing to have Mom with us. But Sue and I have compared notes. The day-to-day physical duties were easy compared to the emotional weight of her care. Only those who have been through a similar situation will understand. I can only describe it as a low-lying cloud of responsibility that never breaks for the sun.

Mom was pleasant. She rarely complained or made unrealistic demands. I knew not to talk with her about my personal life, but I could not overlook the reality that she lived in my personal space. She spent her days in my family room, overheard every conversation, knew my schedule, and witnessed every interaction. But we almost never discussed any of it.

Mom's presence also affected my family. I can honestly say I think it was a good thing Kent traveled. I cannot tell his story, but I know that having grown up with his grandmother, and then having my mom in our home must have been a challenge. As Kent knew they would, Mom's needs came before his. He struggled most with our lack of privacy. For the two months when she was with us, I could never leave, and we couldn't make any plans. Mom also went through a time when she could not stay warm. Though it was the middle of summer, she wanted the pellet stove on with the hot air blowing. The thermostat on the other end of the house registered 85 degrees and she was still cold. Kent developed terrible migraines and the kids melted. I tried an electric blanket, but Mom preferred the pellet stove. After days of watching my family suffer from the heat, I finally had to tell Mom we couldn't physically tolerate the conditions. From then on, we covered her from the neck down in an electric blanket turned on high. She was still cold. By the end of the day, she couldn't wait to lie down in bed.

At night she was hot. In the middle of the night she would call out my name. I was too exhausted to wake, but Kent would hear her and nudge me until I woke. Without fail, I found her drenched in sweat. Her hair was so damp it stuck to her face, and her night shirt and sheets were as wet as if they had just come out of the washer. Invariably, Mom needed help with her breathing. Something would be stuck that she couldn't cough out. I tipped her over the side of the bed and percussed her chest until it dislodged. "Take off the covers," she begged.

I knew she was dying. This body of hers responded in such dramatic ways to her change of position. By the time morning came, she couldn't wait to get out of bed. My heart broke for her. She lived a life void of comfort. Every time I pushed back the wet hair from her agonized face, I wondered if I was looking into my own eyes.

Andrew was three and woke up every day with a bout of crying. I think it was due to stomach pains or allergies. Once he was up and had eaten, he was fine. Janice was five and a going machine. She had projects on any given day that could easily fill a week. My having to take care of Mom drastically impacted her plans. She quickly learned to entertain herself and her friends in our basement.

I noticed she kept her distance from Mom. As I thought about what to do, I decided I wouldn't force the kids to help or be close with Mom. I didn't want them to resent her or me. Mom also had a limited comfort capacity. The kids couldn't sit on her lap due to the pressure it put on her sores. They couldn't move any part of her body or it caused her pain. Sometimes Janice and Mom would have popcorn parties where Janice would sit on the arm of her chair and feed her popcorn.

Janice and Andrew were kind to Mom and patient with me, especially when they needed something and I was busy. But I often wondered about their memories. I had wanted to stay home to give them good memories. This is why I was concerned about the tone of emotion in our home. Even though I felt an overwhelming weight, I didn't want to pass it on to my kids.

When Mom left to go back to Sue's, I spent the first week recovering from exhaustion. Even though it was stable, I also had a brain tumor. I never had the energy to do special things around the holidays or plan vacations. We had abbreviated birthdays and lived in a smaller world and on a smaller scale.

My love and appreciation for Sue's willingness to shoulder this burden grew. When Mom left for Sue's, I couldn't help but think about my sister everyday and pray she would have the strength and energy to meet the demand. Whether Mom was with me or at Sue's, I could not get past the feeling that I was, once again, tangled up in knots.

19

ELCARIM

Kent and I knew Mom would not be with us forever, and I was now in my 30s. Though Mom's care was the focus of our energy and she had lived with us for about two and a half years, our thoughts returned to our own family and if we should have any more children. The question became a matter of sincere prayer. Though I did not receive an overwhelming witness that we should have another child, I could not shake the feeling that our family was not yet complete. Kent felt likewise. When we made the decision we would have another child, we felt calm.

Once again, I did not tell Mom when I found out I was pregnant. I wondered if it was because my attention was so distracted, but I did not carve out my life for this child as I had with Janice and Andrew. When I was pregnant with them, I often found myself thinking into our connected futures. How old would I be when they started kindergarten? What interests would I help them develop? How would I feel when they graduated from high school? With this new pregnancy, I couldn't. Whenever I tried to think of our joined futures, my mind had no wings. I would say to myself, "Maybe after the ultrasound, when I've seen the baby, I'll have some vision."

I didn't tell anyone I was pregnant either. Kent knew, and so did his parents, but that was all. Whenever I considered that I ought to tell so-and-so, I would say to myself again, "Uh, I'll wait until after the ultrasound."

The day of the ultrasound came. I scheduled it for a time when Mom would be with Sue. I figured I was about sixteen weeks along and I was beginning to show. Since Kent was out of town, I took his mother with me, whom I loved dearly. The technician spread the warm jelly over my abdomen and began pushing the transducer like a shovel over my child. I watched the shadowy apparition on the screen. My heart beat faster.

The technician put down the transducer and took a deep breath. "There is something wrong with this baby."

I think I must have expected it. I took a reading and felt no change in my emotion. Perhaps I had received alarming news so frequently, it no longer affected me. I nodded, waiting for her to continue.

She picked up the transducer with one hand, pointing at the screen with the other. "Do you see these shadows here on the sides of the head? Those are cysts most commonly seen in a condition known as Trisomy X. This baby is a girl, and she has three X chromosomes instead of two."

I listened and watched as she moved the transducer over an area of quick movement.

"The biggest problem is here in the heart. She has a very serious heart defect." She put the transducer down again and wiped the jelly off my belly with a towel.

I took a reading again, and still no emotion. No shock, no sorrow, nothing. "Okay," I said.

"I'm sure you have some questions. I'll have you talk with the doctor."

Even as I dressed, I felt nothing. Surely I loved this child, didn't I? Shouldn't I be feeling something?

Betty and I waited in the doctor's office. "Thank you for coming," I told her.

When he came in, the doctor pulled his chair closer and leaned in toward me. "Your child has a genetic mutation known as Trisomy X. We don't know why it happens, but there are two types. One is a fluke of nature and there is no additional risk in subsequent pregnancies. The other is a genetic predisposition and carries an additional risk of this occurring in future pregnancies. I cannot tell you for certain what type your child has; however, when this happens as a fluke of nature, the mutations are far more severe. From looking at your ultrasound, I would guess yours is a fluke of nature. Your child has a severe heart defect. I do not give her any chance of surviving."

For the first time, something registered. "Will she live to be born?"

He shook his head. "I would say there is a 97 percent chance she will not live to term, and if she lives that long, I give her no chance of surviving a delivery. In fact, I'm quite surprised she has lived even this long. Most fetuses with this severe of a defect would have miscarried within the first few weeks. You would never have even known you were pregnant."

Yes, I recognized that feeling again of complete dread. I reminded myself to breathe and nodded my head in acknowledgement of what he'd told me.

"I noticed from your chart," he continued, "that you are LDS. I happen to be a bishop, and in these circumstances, where there is no chance of survival and the carrying of the child presents a risk to you as the mother, this is a situation where an abortion would be an acceptable option. You need to think about this and meet with your OB." (A bishop is an unpaid ecclesiastical leader of a ward. He is a lay member and generally has a regular occupation in addition to his church assignment.)

As the doctor left the room, I experienced the strangest sensation. When I was baptized into the Church and my Uncle Jack lifted me out of the water, I felt the Holy Ghost enter my heart. As the doctor left the room, the Holy Spirit left me. Like a vacuum, it vacated my entire body. I felt small and empty. There was no peace, no whispers, only spiritual silence.

I don't recall saying much to Betty on the ride home. I was lost in my own thoughts. I didn't have to make a decision about whether or not I would have an abortion. I already knew what I was going to do. I was a mother. I would do whatever I could to help this little girl live. I knew with my diagnosis of VHL that continuing with the pregnancy would be a risk, but I also believed in miracles. Perhaps God would give us a miracle.

As the day wore on, the doctor's words repeated themselves over and over in my mind. Though I had not planned our lives together, I still grieved there would be no birthday, no extra plate at our table, no additional Christmas stocking to fill. Without even trying, I had already included her in our family.

As my sense of loss deepened, I became more confused about why the Spirit had left me, especially at this time when I needed Him the most. When Kent arrived home, I asked him for a priesthood blessing. Maybe he would be able to tell me what was going on. I realized that in almost every situation, I had a sense of how things would turn out. I was always being prepared for the outcome. But without the Spirit now, I had no idea of how things would finish.

The first thing Kent counseled me in the blessing he gave was that I needed to be cheerful. He spent a great deal of time telling me that whether I realized it or not, I was an influence. Other people took strength from how I faced my trials. I wasn't going through this just for myself but for others as well. It was important that I be cheerful.

The next thing he told me was that it was not God's will that I should know the outcome of this situation. I needed to learn to walk by faith and live each day trusting in Him.

The last thing Kent focused on was that through this challenge I would receive great wisdom. I would receive insight and knowledge. This experience would be a blessing in my life.

I pondered these themes. Regarding cheerfulness, I thought about the time when I had given Janice a piece of licorice when she was a baby. When I had taken it away, afraid she might choke, she'd been unhappier than if I had never given her the licorice in the first place. At that time, I had promised God that if he ever took something away from me, I wouldn't be angry. I would be grateful for the time I had been given. I didn't know how long I would have with this baby, but I would be grateful for every moment.

The blessing also focused on a theme of faith. My scripture study became a concentrated study on faith. Over the next several weeks I had a difficult time sleeping. I found myself waking in the middle of the night and spending hours on my knees in the closet. The Spirit was still withdrawn. I couldn't reach anybody. I did want God's will, but how could I pray when I didn't know what to pray for? I decided that if God wasn't going to tell me what His will was then I would pray for a miracle. I knew this little child wanted to survive. She had already beaten the odds. I prayed God would heal her.

That's when I began my journey of faith and met up with the brother of Jared in the book of Ether from the *Book of Mormon*. I'd met him many times before, but this time was different. I didn't just brush past him, trying to keep my steady pace. I felt the need to journey with him and learn through his experience.

I envied his relationship with the Savior. By the time I met up with him, this relationship had already been established and I didn't get to see what he'd gone through to develop this closeness, but whenever there was a problem, he talked with the Lord through prayer. Their relationship was such that whenever the brother of Jared prayed, the Lord answered. The answer was clear and the brother of Jared understood it plainly as if they were holding a conversation. I wanted to feel that. I wanted the ability to communicate with the Lord in the same way as the brother of Jared.

I listened in on his prayers. He let me experience with him what it's like to converse with the Lord. I noticed a contrast between his prayers and mine. He was direct and specific; but he was also humble. He frequently asked the Lord not to be angry with him. That affected me. In my own prayers, I asked God not to be angry with me as I persisted in asking for my miracle. Would He please allow my little girl to live?

Though I received no recognizable response to my own prayers, I experienced with the brother of Jared an answer to his. The scripture reads:

> When the brother of Jared had said his words, behold, the Lord stretched forth his hand . . . And the veil was taken from off the eyes of the brother of Jared and he saw the finger of the Lord... He saith unto the Lord: I saw the finger of the Lord, . . . And the Lord said unto him: Because of thy faith thou hast seen . . . Believest thou the words which I shall speak? And he answered: Yea, Lord, I know that thou speakest the truth, for thou art a God of truth, and canst not lie. And when he had said these words, behold, the Lord showed himself unto him, and said . . . Behold, I am he who was prepared from the foundation of the world to redeem my people. Behold, I am Jesus Christ. I am the Father and the Son. In me shall all mankind have life, and that eternally, even they who shall believe on my name; and they shall become my sons and daughters." (Ether 3:6-14)

I saw the Savior, Jesus Christ, through the brother of Jared's eyes. I heard His voice through the brother of Jared's ears. I knew it was true. God had answered the brother of Jared. This experience gave me great strength, especially as Mom moved back in with us.

I did not tell Mom I was pregnant. Her physical condition was deteriorating. Though she hardly complained, I could see the constant pain in her eyes. She was also recovering from a fractured femur. When she had been with me on the previous round, we were at Nanny's family cabin in Island Park and I had taken her for a ride. At one point, she needed me to help her get some fluid out of her lungs. I pulled over, hopped out of the car, and was tipping her over my leg to percuss her back when we both heard a loud pop. I worried I had popped one of her hips out of joint. I felt both hips and they felt normal. Mom didn't register any pain, no change, nothing. We finished our ride and went about the day as usual. When we put her to bed that night, her thigh was in two pieces. The skin was intact, but it was clear her femur had broken in half.

I nearly fainted. Normally when someone even fractures a femur (let alone breaks it into two) the pain is unbearable. There is a huge amount of swelling and potential for hemorrhaging and tissue damage. Mom registered no pain, and there was absolutely no swelling. Her years of immobility had left her bones weak and brittle.

When I took her to the emergency room in Idaho Falls, I figured they'd probably haul me off for elder abuse. Thank goodness Mom could communicate well. They immobilized the femur and instructed me to take her home where she could receive treatment. The amazing part for me was this recognition—if a broken femur was not painful, the pain she experienced on a daily basis must have been excruciating.

One day she moaned about pain in her tooth. She wasn't normally demanding, but on this occasion she insisted I call the dentist, who was also a personal friend, and take her in that day. Kent was out of town. "Could I take you in tomorrow when Kent is here and he could help me?"

"I have to go today."

At this stage in my pregnancy, lifting Mom was not in the best interest of my baby. I knew that. But given Mom's insistence and complaints of pain, I said a prayer and made the appointment. With two small children in tow, I lifted her from her chair to the wheelchair then from the wheelchair to the car. Once we arrived at the dentist, I transferred her from the car to her wheelchair, lifting her in the chair up a flight of stairs into the office and then transferred her into the dentist's chair. At the end of her procedure, she was flat on her back and getting her into the wheelchair would be a dead lift. I asked the dentist if he would lift Mom for me. He backed away, "I'm sure you are better at that."

I couldn't blame him. Mom's body was rigid and contorted. Her difficulty with breathing made it obvious she was in pain. Not to mention, she was still recovering from a broken femur.

I took a deep breath and lifted Mom into her wheelchair. She stared me down, and I knew she was angry. I knew it would bother her that I had asked her friend the dentist to help. She wouldn't speak to me on the way home. I transferred her from the car to the chair, lifted her up the front steps in her wheelchair then lifted her back into her reclining chair in the family room. After the kids went to bed, I sat down by Mom's chair.

"Mom," I told her, "I am pregnant."

Her eyes softened and her jaw relaxed as she realized why I had hesitated to take her without Kent's help and why I had asked the dentist to help lift her. "Do you think the baby will be okay?"

I winced and took in a slow breath. "The baby is sick, and they don't expect her to live."

The color in Mom's face flushed out. "Is that because of lifting me today?"

"Oh, no," I assured her. "That had nothing to do with it. She's always been sick. But I still feel a need to protect and take care of her."

That was the end of the conversation. When I stood, Mom said, "You are an angel."

That was the first compliment I ever remember her giving me.

I was still pregnant when Mom left to go back to Sue's in December of 1993. This little girl, we named Angela, had passed a critical point in time. For whatever reason, society had determined that up until twenty weeks, a fetus is not a person. Since Angela had lived longer than this twenty-week period, she was officially ours and could be considered our child. I knew every day I had with her was a gift. I lived with the constant awareness that inside of me, in that place where life begins, my baby was dying. This was her struggle. I could not do anything to help her, except eat, breathe, and pray.

I burrowed my distress in, as you would tuck an overhanging bed sheet under the mattress, where it couldn't be noticed. Otherwise, I could not have functioned, or even had the capacity to carry on a coherent conversation. But challenges with this much emotional charge, though hidden, are not quiet. All that worry, heartbreak, and horror churned, thrashing like a tormented sleeper for a comfortable position where it could rest.

The sweet story of a woman began coming to me. My soul needed a soft place to idle, and in thinking of her story, I found peace.

My mind's need for escape reminded me of when I had taken care of a grand old woman in a care facility when I was in nursing school. I took care of her for three days and made arrangements to do a follow-up visit after she went home. When I arrived at her apartment after her discharge, she did not remember me. She told me that for the whole time she was in the care facility, her mind had taken a "fabulous vacation."

I look back on this experience of my own mind taking a vacation and see it as an exercise in "receiving." But the story of this young woman I came to know as "Claire" unfolded as the days went by. Just as composers who after writing a magnificent symphony state simply, "I heard the music in my head," her story unfolded in my mind as though I were watching a movie.

As I waited for the death of my child, in mindless moments, such as when washing dishes or vacuuming, my mind returned to the peace of this young woman's story, wanting to know what became of her. She was born in 1917 and loved gardening. Claire was unassuming and endearing. One of the things I loved most about her was her ability to find meaning in simple things. Every plant represented something dear to her, and the seasons of life unlocked mysteries. This "revelation" of my fictional friend became a soothing and powerful escape.

Back in my real life, I faced another difficulty. I was beginning to show and could no longer fit into any of my regular clothes. At a ward Christmas party, one of my sweet neighbors asked if I was pregnant. I didn't know how to answer. Under normal circumstances, pregnancy is a happy occasion. I couldn't bring myself to pretend mine was. "Yes," I told her, "but they don't expect the baby to live. That's why I haven't mentioned it."

I saw her, a few minutes later, being comforted in the arms of her husband. It was another confirmation that my experience did impact other people.

About a week later, I began spotting. I left the kids home with Kent and went to the hospital. An ultrasound confirmed Angela had died. There would be no miracle for her.

Throughout my life, I had discovered living with emotions to be similar to swimming in water. Over the years, I had learned to swim close to the surface where it was easier to breathe. But on this day, I plunged deep. For several hours after managing to drive home, I found myself gasping for air.

It was Saturday, and my OB would not be back until Monday. The weekend was torture, knowing that my dead child was inside of me. I was not cheerful.

Angela was delivered on December 14, 1993. The nurse handed me a pamphlet entitled, "When the Womb Is a Tomb." I held her body in my palms and thanked her for being with me, for fighting so hard, and for the blessing she had been in my life. Her tiny body felt more like soft clay than flesh and bones. She had survived long enough in the womb that we could be given a death certificate and bury her body. She was our child and belonged to us. She was now a part of our family.

When the question of where we should bury her arose, Kent's mother approached us. She and Kent's father had burial plots in the Salt Lake City Cemetery and she had already called.

"If it's okay with you, I'd like Angela to be buried with me. They can put her in my place for now, and when I pass away, they can place her casket on top of mine. I would be honored to have Angela with me."

In Claire's story, this tender character who calmed my thoughts, Claire shared a special bond with her own grandmother. I couldn't think of a more loving and suitable place for Angela to rest than with her grandmother.

Kent and I went together to the mortuary to dress Angela. The mortician handed us a small Ziploc bag, and I pulled out a beautiful white dress so small it could have fit a doll. There was also a cap and small footies for Angela's feet. Inside was a note, "Made with love for you by sisters in the Relief Society." I mention this hoping one day they will know how greatly I appreciated their gift.

I just needed to hold her. Looking at her small and defective body, I had a better understanding of the struggle she had endured. It was a miracle she lived so long. I brushed my thumb across her cold cheek and was once again reminded of the licorice lesson. In those few moments, as I recommitted myself to being grateful for the time I had been given, Angela and I bonded. Her spirit wasn't in that body anymore, but she was there.

Another miracle took place in those few moments. Kent would tell me later something happened to him in that room. He would never look at me the same. Though he had *always* been supportive and committed in our marriage, his heart was softened even more towards me. From that time on, he treated me with an extra measure of tenderness.

Angela was buried on December 16, 1993, the day of our tenth wedding anniversary. She is resting there in her grandmother's space knowing she is wanted and loved.

I reflected on my life at this time and how it seemed my life was an elcarim, the opposite of a miracle. In many ways, nature had combined against the odds to create the worst possible outcome. My father had not just been in a plane accident, he had died in a midair collision. My mother did not just have a disease, she had a rare genetic disorder, one that I had inherited. And now I had not just lost a child, she had died of yet another rare genetic anomaly, completely different from the one I already had. What were the odds?

Fifteen years have passed since then, and I am beginning to see things in a different light. Elcarim is *miracle* spelled backwards. As I look back, I begin to see things I hadn't seen before. In the blessing Kent gave me, he told me my experience with Angela would be a great blessing in my life. Though I couldn't see it then, I am beginning to see it now. Perhaps my life is an elcarim, and I will only see the miracle of it all as I view my life from the end to the beginning.

20

PREPARING FOR CHRISTMAS

After we buried Angela on December 16, 1993, I prepared for Christmas. Janice was now four and Andrew had just turned three at the end of November. My body began recovering from an unfruitful harvest. Despite taking medication to prevent the natural production of infant nourishment, in a sad irony, on the day when we celebrated the birth of a living child, my milk poured in anyway. For several days, I suffered a visceral and painful reminder of Angela's absence. Amidst these feelings of grief and mourning, more thoughts of Claire seeped in. The details of her story soothed me. One night, after the kids went to bed, my brain seemed so full of millions of tidbits of information, I decided to write some of them down. The release of her story to a page liberated my mind, and I experienced a noticeable relief of physical tension. As I wrote and reread what I had written, it became obvious I had no context or understanding of the times she lived in.

One of my favorite scriptures is found in the Book of Mormon, 1 Nephi 17:13, where the Lord says, "I will also be your light in the wilderness; and I will prepare the way before you, . . . inasmuch as ye shall keep my commandments, ye shall be led towards the promised land; and ye shall know that it is by me that ye are led."

Loss is such an abrupt ending. This loss forced me to acknowledge life could not, and would not, ever be the same. Though it might seem a paradox, this imposed surrender to circumstances beyond my power actually created a powerful momentum for change. As a child, this momentum resulted in an all-consuming vortex of fear that swallowed me back into myself. I recognize this same process in others who become angry and bitter.

In Angela's case, my reminder of what little power I had over my own life freed me. After losing so much throughout my life, what more did I have to fear? I entered the wilderness and waited for the Lord's light to guide me to a better place.

Claire is really the story of how I was led out of despair into a brighter, richer world. This occurred through a process of synchronicity –coincidences that led me to the next step.

After Angela's passing and my awareness that I knew nothing about the times my fictional Claire lived in, there was a change in my visiting teaching assignment. I was asked to visit Klea, an older sister in the ward who "happened" to be born in 1917. This was the same year Claire had been born as well. My new visiting teaching partner was Edna, who was born a few years after Klea.

I became an interested student of their lives and experiences. As Klea and Edna discussed the times and culture of their youth, events and attitudes in Claire's life began making sense. Our discussions left me wanting to know more, and I began daytrips to the Marriott Library at the University of Utah to check out books, magazines, and newspapers relating to the time period of Claire's life. I listened to hundreds of radio shows from that time, including *The Jack Benny Program, The Burns and Allen Show,* and *Fibber McGee & Molly.* I checked out books on plant lore and legend. Once again, I was astounded by how closely Claire's thoughts about plants paralleled what I was reading.

I studied Finnish history and culture and read the *Kalevala,* a book of Finnish folklore that told a beautiful story of aged heroes. Claire's grandmother had emigrated from Finland, and I recognized so much of her outlook on life from that work.

I researched a thousand topics and became a voracious reader on anything that had to do with Claire's interests or the era in which she lived. This process changed me. My life expanded beyond my own little world. Though I had lost Angela, I read about thousands of children who died each year of polio and diphtheria. And when I shuddered at how emaciated my mother's body had become, I only had to look at documented photos from the Holocaust to see thousands upon thousands of bodies similar to hers. I now had something to compare my life to. I had a little bigger perspective.

I also became more interested in others. Rather than falling into my own whirlpool of sorrow and grief, I wanted to know about other people's experiences. I developed a love for learning and felt a force building in my spirit that pushed me forward.

When Mom came back to stay with me, I was a different person. So was she. Virginia and Suzanne, her visiting teachers, had continued their weekly visits with Mom, reading the scriptures and discussing spiritual matters. Mom had softened. She believed their words and had reconciled herself with God. He was her friend now. There were times after her visits with Virginia and Suzanne when she would continue the discussion with me and I knew her heart had changed.

One day she told Kent, "If I didn't have this disease, I would have been a completely different person."

When Kent asked, "How so?" She explained, "I think I would have been very materialistic. I know I would have been a social climber."

She had reconciled her life and condition. We were witnesses.

I should have known this would be the last time she would be with me. Every time she came for our two months I wondered how long she would live, but it had been almost three and a half years since Sue and I had taken her into our homes and after that long, I figured there would always be another turn in two months' time.

There were signs she was failing. Her nights became more restless. Kent would wake me to her cries, but now when I went in to clap her chest, she was delirious. She would be wide-eyed but vacant, talking nonsense to the invisible. On these nights, I sat down on the floor by her bed and hugged my knees until she returned and noticed me there. "Hey, could you pound this stuff out of my chest?" she would ask.

"Sure." I lowered her head over the side of the bed and moved my cupped hands over her ribs.

She was also much calmer. That agonized look in her eyes diminished, and she spent more of her daytime hours sleeping in the chair. Also, foods tasted different to her. Some nights after I cooked a dish she'd eaten a hundred times she'd say, "What did you put in this, it's awful." It tasted just the same to me as it had the previous hundred times. Something was changing.

I will always be grateful to Nanny and Aunt Joyce who came to stay with Mom every Friday so I could go up to the library and continue my studies. They continued their faithful and loyal support of Mom, even following her move from Bountiful. By this time, Janice was in school and Andrew had preschool along with an afternoon playgroup. In my treks to the library, I finally found common ground with Mom. She also loved to learn. We talked history, books, and discussed great thoughts. Mom had a brilliant, vibrant mind and expressed profound insights. I often went to bed marveling that even as her body continued deteriorating, her mind and spirit soared. How sorry I was that I had not drawn from her wisdom sooner. She had a unique perspective of experience, and after her passing, I considered it one of my greatest losses that I had not tapped more into the wealth of her character. Unfortunately, she took most of it with her. We will never know how she coped with the deterioration of her physical body without complaint or murmuring. Nor will we understand what it is like to lose everything, be completely dependent on everyone else, and still find the motivation to get out of bed each and every morning.

Rob came out to be with Mom over Mother's Day in 1995. This was the first time he had specifically come out alone to spend time with Mom. Since Mom was back with Sue, Rob stayed out there as well. Sue was asked to speak about Mom for Mother's Day in her ward, which she did. Though Mom could not make the service, Sue read her the talk. Rob had some alone-time with Mom as well. One morning while Rob was there, I got a call from Sue. "Mom's not putting out any urine in her catheter. The aide changed the catheter this morning, but there's still no urine."

Mom's kidneys were shutting down. Sue and I both took a deep breath. All of these years Mom had been with us, she had given us strict instructions, "No doctors." Given all of her physical problems, she saw a urologist once a year to get a prescription for a preventive antibiotic and that was her only appointment.

"What should we do?" Sue asked.

We both knew she needed immediate attention, but would taking her to the doctor help, or just prolong her suffering?

My views on suffering were colored by my experiences as a nurse caring for terminal patients, as well as my belief that death is not just a birth into another world but a birth into a better world. Death did not frighten me, but I had been a witness to the terrible suffering associated with the process of dying. I was constantly disturbed by the medical horrors we inflict on terminal patients in an effort to give them more time.

Life support is very painful. Many patients had to be induced into a coma to tolerate the discomfort of the tubes and the machine's function. Was this "time?" Almost every medical procedure involves suffering and a long list of possible complications. For terminal patients, where they will not return to a full and healthy life, why do we add insult to their injury? So many of my cancer patients, as they prepared to pass over, would say to me, "If I knew what I know now, when they gave me the diagnosis, I would have said, 'thank you,' and enjoyed the rest of my life instead of ruining that precious time being sick from the treatment."

I will never forget the day I walked in to take care of an Alzheimer's patient receiving IV antibiotics for a bladder infection. This gentleman's wrists and ankles were strapped to the bed to prevent him from leaving or pulling out the IV. He was thrashing and moaning trying to free himself. I placed my hand on his chest. He immediately settled, and when he looked at me, I could see from his eyes he had once been a dignified someone. It broke my heart we had degraded him to this, in the name of treatment, instead of allowing nature to take its merciful course.

Now it was my mom. She had suffered so many years already.

Sue went on. "Rob wants to take her to the emergency room. That's what the aide suggested." I sensed the dilemma in her voice.

"This is your call," I told her. "I will support you in whatever you decide is best."

I got the call that Mom was at Alta View Emergency Room. Since her oxygen saturation was low, they had put her on oxygen. They started an IV and gave her fluids and some medication to help her urinary output. With that they sent her home.

Sue called me a few hours later, desperate. "They didn't send Mom home with the oxygen, and now she wants us to take her back because she says she can't breathe. Rob wants to take her right now."

"I'll be right out," I told her.

When I arrived at Sue's house, Mom's coloring looked as pale as it always had. She had probably been oxygen deprived for months and just didn't know it until they gave her oxygen in the emergency room. If we were to take her back to the hospital, where would it lead? I didn't want Mom to suffer anymore. For some reason, as a society we think medicine has all the answers and will painlessly solve everything. I knew differently, and I just wanted Mom to be comfortable.

"Take me back to the hospital," Mom demanded.

I nodded my head. "We can do that, Mom, but right now is an important time for you to make some decisions. The reality is—your body is shutting down. It has served you all these years and it is now saying it has had enough. We can take you to the hospital, Mom, but here's what's going to happen. They will put you back on oxygen, but after a little while, that won't be enough, then they'll put you on a mask. When that's not enough, they'll put a tube down your throat or give you a tracheotomy and put you on a respirator. Same with your kidneys. They can put you on fluids and medications, but when that stops working, they'll hook you up to a dialysis machine. Same with your heart. With each one of these steps, you will experience the pain of dying all over again. You need to ask yourself, Mom, how many times you want to suffer the pain of dying."

Her jaw stiffened. "Susan, Rob, take me to the hospital now." She looked at me, "You don't ever need to come and see me again."

I nodded with regret, "We will comply with your wishes."

Kent and I were scheduled to go to dinner with some of our dear friends. The husband was a physician and the wife was a nurse. The two of them were such a support as I told them about Mom's situation and my dilemma. Their empathy calmed me.

As Kent and I walked in the door from dinner, the phone rang. The voice on the other end identified herself as Mom's nurse at the hospital. "Your mother asked me to call. She said to tell you, you were right and asked that you come see her tonight."

"I'll be right there."

When I walked in, Mom was delirious, oxygen hissing in her nasal canula.

"I'm here," I whispered.

Her vacant eyes stared in my direction. I waited for her to return. I realized now she had been dying for months, each system accommodating itself to a little less function, similar to the diminishing hours of sunshine as the season moves closer to winter.

"You were right," Mom said when her eyes registered. "The oxygen wasn't enough. They've turned it up several times already, and it's still not enough. What should I do?"

"You get to decide when you've had enough."

Without any hesitation, she told me, "I've had enough."

I looked over her IV tubing with little bags piggybacked into her main line for different medications. If there was any hope she would get better, it would have been different, but she wouldn't be getting any better. "Maybe tomorrow we should get rid of all this stuff."

Mom nodded. "First thing in the morning." She took a deep breath, "Thank you. Thank you for everything."

I couldn't stop staring. All those years I had waited to hear those words. I had been taking care of her since I was fourteen. I was now thirty-two. I smiled at how easily she said, "Thank you."

I knew she couldn't feel it, but I took her hand. "I love you, Mom."

Her eyes turned vacant again. I sat by her bed, holding her hand until the nurse came in at 5:00 A.M. to get her vitals. Mom was still delirious. The nurse took the blood pressure with the cuff. She shook her head, telling me she couldn't get anything, and then brought in the machine. When the alarm beeped, we both jumped to see the reading of 50/30. With healthy people, anything under 70 systolic is generally life threatening. Though incoherent, Mom was still breathing. No wonder she was delirious. All of these months, her blood pressure must have been dropping at night.

Since Mom had the IV, they opened the bag and let the fluids run in. Within twenty minutes, Mom was back and lucid. I suppose every organ in her body was so used to having nothing, she could live on a blood pressure of 50/30. I couldn't believe her tenacity. When I knew she was okay, and Mom had fallen back to sleep, I left for home to get some sleep.

Sue came early. She and Mom met with the social worker and agreed to pull the IV and all the medications. Mom asked to keep the oxygen. Sue called me, "ML, I just can't do it. This oxygen stuff will put me over the edge. I can't handle having to deal with all of this at home. Since we're essentially taking her off everything, they won't keep her in the hospital. The social worker said we could look at some care facilities today, but we have to move her tomorrow."

I understood Sue's concern, especially given how upset Mom had become about her oxygen when Sue had taken her home from the emergency room. We made arrangements for a care facility the next day. Mom wasn't happy, but we explained her care had gone beyond our ability. We wanted her to be comfortable.

Mom spent the day calling all of her friends. She knew she didn't have long but didn't say a word about that. "Just calling to check in," is how she started each conversation.

I told Sue how Mom had finally said, "Thank you," and encouraged her to spend the night with Mom so they could have some time together.

At 5:00 A.M. the next morning, Sue called me. "Mom's blood pressure is 50/30. You might want to come in."

"She did this last night, too. If anyone can pull through this, Mom can." I was exhausted, but this time, Mom didn't have an IV. I told Sue, "I'm on my way."

By the time I reached the hospital, Mom was gone. I'm glad Sue was with her. When we called her friends to let them know, they all said the same thing, "But I just talked with her yesterday, and she sounded fine."

Elisabeth Kubler-Ross, a renowned expert in the field of death and dying, has written that after someone dies, loved ones experience a kind of euphoria. I definitely experienced this. If I understood her correctly, Kubler-Ross explained this feeling as a relief for the ones left behind that they are still alive.

The euphoria I experienced was more powerful than any human emotion of relief. It had the manifestation of a spiritual nature, as if I were being given a taste of the joy Mom felt when she was freed from her prison-body. Sue felt it also. Even though Mom had been so afraid to die, we both knew she was fine now. We shared in her joy.

I expected to feel some relief, a sense of that heavy cloud of responsibility being lifted from my shoulders, but there was one emotional adjustment I was not prepared for. Taking care of Mom gave me an important purpose. After Mom died, my life didn't feel quite as significant. I saw how the giving of service had magnified my life. In a way, my burden gave me worth.

I also think the euphoria was heaven's recognition of a life well-led. As I have gone through my own experiences, raising teenagers, having surgeries, discovering this disease in my own child, I often reflect on Mom and wonder how she did it all on her own. She overcame incredible challenges with courage and dignity.

Also meshed inside of that amazing feeling was the love I gained for my sister, Sue. We shared a sacred bond of responsibility, and I couldn't have done it without her. She gave Mom her best, and it was sweet, and kind, and tender. Mom never wanted for anything when she was with Sue. That's why it broke my heart when Sue had to go through the caring for a loved one all over again so soon after Mom died.

At the back of my own copy of Kubler-Ross's *On Death and Dying*, I wrote, "We are aware of all we leave behind but have no idea of what we have to look forward to." Maybe that's also what Sue and I experienced after Mom died—some idea of what we have to look forward to.

21

FAITH

There is at least one major regret I have from my life. Sue called a day or two after Mom's funeral to ask if I would come over and help her go through Mom's things. I couldn't do it. Mom had truly given up everything by the time she died. She had absolutely nothing of personal value. Everything that remained was a reminder of her illness—the cushion with air pump she sat on every day, catheter supplies for her bladder, dressings and bandages for her deep bed sores, clothes that were easy to get on and off her paralyzed body, the tape recorder with tapes loaned to her from the blind center, and her wheelchair. I still feel terrible I made Sue dispose of all of that on her own. I should have been there to help.

Sue took care of Mom's things before she and Russ decided to take a week's vacation and go to the cabin. They left for the cabin the week after Mom died. Neither Sue nor I had taken a vacation for three years. We really couldn't take one while Mom was with us, and when Mom spent her two months away, neither of us had the energy to plan, let alone go on a vacation.

When Sue had been gone a few days, she called. She and Russ had been working on a log project, and Russ had had a stroke. He was forty-three. They had life-flighted him to Idaho Falls, and Sue was on her way there. It didn't look good.

If you are at this moment thinking, "Hang on, this is too much. I can't handle hearing about one more tragedy," you know exactly how I felt.

I hung up the phone stunned. How on earth could this be? Hadn't Sue been through enough already? Mom had only been gone one week.

I am deeply aware this is Sue and Russ's story to tell. They lived every moment, and if I tried to tell their story, I would get it wrong and miss all of those nuances that give it life and all of those details that give it meaning. I only want to tell how their experience affected me, and what I learned.

As I drove up to Idaho Falls, I talked with God the whole way. I kept asking Him, "How strong is my faith?" I believed faith precedes a miracle. Did I have enough faith to bring about a miracle for my sister and her husband? And this wasn't just some random question flung out into the universe. I expected a specific answer.

As I passed Ogden and then Tremonton, I tried to remember, was it ever said in the scriptures that the strength of our faith was to remain a mystery? What about the story of Lehi and the Liahona in the Book of Mormon? Lehi and his family had a way of measuring their faith. Every morning, they could look at that little brass ball of curious workmanship that worked like a compass, according to their faith, and know exactly how strong their faith was. I wanted some gauge or apparatus similar to a battery tester that I could plug in any time and know the exact strength of my faith. At the time, it did not seem an unreasonable request.

I met Sue in the hospital, and she took me into Russ's room in the Neuro Intensive Care Unit. Russ looked at me and nodded with recognition, but he couldn't speak. The words just wouldn't come. In frustration, he lifted his left hand out to me instead. He couldn't move anything on his right side. I took his hand.

I don't remember what was said, but my heart ached. He was altered, and a whole side of him was dead. Over the next few hours, his brain injury led to the expected, albeit dangerous, increase in swelling. The cranium is not a good expander, and as the swelling increased, Russ relaxed and breathed his way into a coma. Only time would tell if he would live. The swelling would continue for seventy-two hours from the time of his initial injury. He still had about sixty hours to go.

On one occasion, I sat with Sue in his room. She held his hand, cuddled his face, and talked to him in loving tones. His body remained unresponsive. In that eerie stillness, he was struggling for his life.

My chest hurt. It had only been one week since Mom died. Sue had been through too much already. She needed a miracle. She deserved a miracle.

"How strong is my faith?" I asked again.

Russ finally regained consciousness, and they allowed Sue to drive him down to the rehab center in Salt Lake. By this time, he could sit up, but his right side was still dangling. The doctors told Sue that because of the location of his bleed, he might never speak again. He might not understand what anyone said to him either. He might not be able to read or understand written language at all. All of this in addition to the loss of function in his right side. He, of course, happened to be right-handed.

Sue took a deep breath and wheeled Russ out of the hospital. As he settled into the passenger seat of her car, Russ looked at Sue, half of his face smiling. He held out his hand for the keys. Sue smiled back, "No way are you driving!"

The days turned into weeks as Russ and Sue endured the emotional task of determining the extent of his disabilities. As Sue settled into the role of caretaker once again, my unanswered question fell to a whisper in the noise of everyday living.

I'm sure the progress to them must have seemed slow indeed, but two months later, I watched with amazement as Russ, with some assistance, descended the steps into a baptismal font. His daughter Emily held on as he very slowly and with some difficulty pronounced the sacred words of the baptismal ordinance and immersed Emily. I know it was not the miraculous healing I had requested, but I still recognized his ability to baptize Emily as a gift.

Then it came time to plan our own family vacation. Should we extend our two-day excursion, the first one we'd taken in three years, to three days by driving home on Sunday? It didn't seem an earth-revolving decision, we would only miss going to church for one, single week, but into my mind came the words—how strong is your faith?

Over the next several weeks, whenever there was a choice, even if it was as small as what song to listen to on the radio or what television show to watch, those words returned: How strong is your faith?

I finally realized what the Lord was trying to tell me. I didn't need a gauge. I could determine the strength of my faith at any moment. My faith was only as strong as my obedience to the will of the Lord.

For the little I did, I expected so much in return. I'm grateful the Lord was so gentle in His lesson. I now believe that obedience unlocks the power of faith.

Russ did learn how to speak; he could also read, and over time became pretty good with his left hand. He also gained enough function of his right side to walk, drive, and be independent and meet all of his own personal needs.

Even more amazing than the changes that took place in Russ were the changes that took place in Sue. She was the only one out of the three of us who didn't finish college. She had been a dedicated homemaker, mother, and wife. Now their needs had changed. With Russ home, Sue went back to school. She prayed for inspiration about what she should pursue in order to meet the financial needs of her family. Her answer came that she should go into pharmacy. She was an older student taking classes such as biochemistry and physiology with young premed majors. But with each semester behind her, Sue's confidence grew. The tone of her voice became lighter and happier.

I was there the day she graduated with her Pharm.D, her graduate degree in pharmacy from the University of Utah. Nanny, Aunt Joyce, and Uncle Lee were there, along with Russ and the kids, Emily and Jacob. Their son Sam couldn't make it because of an important school activity.

As I watched Sue walk up to receive her diploma, I was so proud of her. I knew Mom was proud of her, too. Once again, Sue had met and overcome an overwhelming challenge. I applauded as a witness of her amazing accomplishment.

Through this experience, I've also come to realize God and I have a different definition of a miracle. When I think of the word *miracle,* I think of a dramatic change in outcome or circumstance. I'm beginning to see God's definition involves a dramatic change in the individuals involved. I see now that Sue was given a miracle. The person she has become is the miracle.

22

BETTER THAN EXPECTED

People are so kind and often ask, "ML, how's your health?"

I usually say the same thing, "Unless someone tells me otherwise, I'm doing great."

That's how it always seems to work. I feel fine, no problems, no symptoms, and I go in for a routine scan. When I meet with the doctor, he's the one who tells me I have a problem.

This is how it happened not long after Mom died. Though I was tired after recovering from Angela's birth and Mom's passing, I felt healthy. I went in for my routine scans and got a call from my urologist.

The moment I heard his voice, I thought, *Dang it.*

"You have another kidney tumor," he told me, "And this one is right in the middle. I'm not sure if we can save your kidney this time. Make an appointment and let's schedule surgery."

Janice was in first grade and I remember lying by her on her bed. "I'm going in for a surgery."

Her eyes got big and watery.

I said, "You know how Grandma Janet was sick—"

She didn't let me finish. She shook her head, horrified, and backed away, "Oh, Mom, I knew it. I wanted to tell you all the time not to get too close to her or you would catch it too. I knew you'd catch it. Now you're sick like Grandma Janet."

My words caught in my throat. All the time Mom had been with us, Janice saw her through kindergarten eyes. Mom's "sickness" had everything to do with germs and hand washing. No wonder Janice had always kept her distance, not wanting to get too close to Mom. I wished I had known.

How was I supposed to explain genetics to a six-year-old? I did my best to explain that I hadn't "caught" Mom's sickness, I had been born with it. It was always inside of me. And because it was inside, no one could catch it from me, either.

I have to take a deep breath here. There have been times in my life when I have been desperate to know how a particular situation would turn out. Whether or not I would or should have children was one of those. Looking back, I also realize there are times when I am grateful I didn't know at the time what the future held. This moment happened to be one of these.

And I'm not sure if I ever convinced Janice she wouldn't catch my disease. She had always been the child that kept her distance, even as a baby. She didn't like to cuddle and rarely allowed me to hold her close. I had to find other ways to express my love. But on this occasion, I wanted her to know why I was going to be gone, and why other people would be caring for her. Andrew was only about four.

When I met with the urologist, he displayed a shadowy picture of my kidney over a light box. He pointed to a dark spot, "Because the tumor is here smack in the middle, I might not be able to save the rest of the kidney."

I was in my 30s and this was the second time I'd had kidney cancer in this same kidney. He didn't have to tell me what this meant. If I lost this whole kidney, I would only have a partial kidney on the other side and a big chance I'd have more tumors in that one too. In my days as a nurse, I took care of kidney patients on dialysis. Their fluid intake was restricted. This was more of a struggle for many of them than changing their diet. Dialysis interrupted their lives, taking roughly three hours for a treatment, and they had to go at least once a week. The patients complained of feeling sick and bloated for a day before dialysis and then feeling drained and limp for a day or two after. They generally felt lucky if they had one good day out of seven. I'm not saying they complained; most were happy to be alive, but I certainly didn't see dialysis as something to look forward to.

The other option was a kidney transplant. The care and outcome for transplant patients has improved dramatically, but at that time, many rejected their donated kidneys. It was enough to lose their own kidney, but when these patients lost someone else's, it was devastating. Especially if the donor was still alive and had gone through the pain of surgery to give their kidney as a gift. Add to that, the medications these patients took to keep from rejecting their kidneys had horrendous side effects. They took massive amounts of steroids, and it showed in their puffy faces, round bodies, mottled skin, and unstable moods. If I were to lose my kidneys, it would be a drastic and difficult road.

Surprisingly, into my mind came these words, *Things will go better than expected.*

This thought came as such an interruption, I knew it wasn't mine. I was too busy preparing for the worst and planning my eventual dialysis schedule. Then the message was repeated, *Things will go better than expected.* This time I felt it. I didn't know exactly what it meant, but I knew it was true.

I think I bowed my head and smiled. I looked at the urologist and almost apologetically told him, "Things will go better than expected."

His eyebrows creased, he studied me for a moment, then said, "Oh, okay."

I was scheduled for surgery the next day.

I figured he considered me a total nut case, and maybe I was, but I had such a feeling of calm. I might be losing my kidney, but whatever happened, I knew it would be okay.

Before the anesthesiologist put me under, the doctor came in and said, "Hello." I was already on the pre-op bed, naked under my hospital gown, my hair neatly tucked up inside one of those blue caps, and my name on a tag around my wrist. I took a deep breath and the next thing I knew, I was waking up groggy and in pain. I had to remind myself I was in the hospital and had just undergone surgery. That's right, and did I still have my kidney?

I felt the doctor's hand on my shoulder. "You did great," he said.

"Do I still have my kidney?" I asked, not sure if I was slurring my words.

"Yes," he answered. He paused for a moment. "Things went better than expected."

Later, when I was more alert, Kent came in. He gave me a soft kiss and said, "ML, I know you are still waking up, but you have to hear the story. After the doctor opened you up, he couldn't find the tumor. He took the kidney out, he felt all over for it, but couldn't tell where it was. He had them bring in all the films, and he agonized over where that tumor was 'cause he couldn't tell. Finally, he decided he'd just have to take a blind stab through your kidney. Well, right where that scalpel stopped, your tumor pushed up through the incision. He was able to scoop it out with hardly any damage to the rest of your kidney. He couldn't believe it. ML, you are one lucky lady."

I couldn't believe it either. Things had gone much better than I ever expected. Later that evening, one of the residents came in. I'd never met her before. She looked too pretty and young to be in medical school, but she shook her head, "You have angels watching over you, you know that?"

She must have been in on the surgery. "Oh, yes." I smiled, "I definitely know that someone is watching out for me. There is no doubt in my mind about that."

I was home in three days and back on the treadmill two weeks later. I experienced very little pain and had no trouble throughout my recovery.

There were some quiet moments when I took the time to thank my Heavenly Father. In my life, I had been through some pretty tough spots, and this was one of the first times where things turned out easier than I anticipated. In addition, ever since the Spirit had left me when I found out Angela was sick, I wondered if I would feel or hear it again. And I'm not exactly certain why it had to leave me in the first place. Maybe I had to pass some test or I had to make my own decisions without knowing how things would turn out. A part of me even wondered if I had done something wrong or offended the Spirit in some way; but for whatever reason it left, I celebrated this experience as a sign that not only was the Spirit back, but it was watching out for me.

I just returned from attending stake conference, a meeting where several wards meet together, and I've been thinking about something our stake president said. President Petersen's Church calling is to preside over the eight wards in our stake, but he also works full-time as a psychiatrist, and in his talk he shared some statistics. Studies have shown people who believe in God are much happier and have a more optimistic outlook on life than those who don't. Ding, ding, ding. I appreciate at least one reason why that would be the case. With God, we know that no matter how tough things are, in the end, they will turn out better than we expected.

23

DESIGNING MY LIFE

Mom had passed away and life settled down for my little family. But before I could turn around, Janice and Andrew both gave me a kiss good-bye and ran off to school. I don't know how that happened so quickly, but in a flash they were out the door and spending more hours in a day with their teachers than they were with me. I had my own life again.

This was actually a difficult adjustment. Whereas before, my house had been stretched too full, it now felt hollow. My thoughts of Claire and her story, this fictional woman born in 1917, filled my emptiness. I continued to study areas of her interests as well as events of her time. With the children at school, the opportunity came to start writing down what I knew about her life. I would sit down at the computer in the morning, and in what seemed like a few minutes, the kids would come running back through the door.

The scriptures often address the question, how do you know if something is good? The answer is often, "by their fruits shall ye know them." Something that is good, produces good fruit. An inner change of heart manifests itself in outward ways. We can judge if a change of heart is good by the way it manifests itself in our lives. I wrote about Claire's life in an effort to refocus my emotional energy in a positive direction. I did not anticipate that the writing of her story would change my life.

As I wrote, I lost all sense of the passage of time and became irritated with small distractions. I snarled if the phone rang, or a knock came at my door. Having been repressed for so many years, I believe the right side of my brain awakened. For the first time in my life, I experienced a delirious passion. This right-sided excitement for writing expressed itself in other ways as well.

As Claire's story unfolded in my mind, she fell in love and eventually married a young man who ended up being an architect. As I studied architecture, my vision changed. Now I noticed textures, patterns, and scale. Vision became a study in light, shadows, and color. I found myself, on one occasion, in the rare books department at the University of Utah Marriott Library reading Ernest A. Batchelder's *Principles of Design*. He published this work in 1904. How I ended up there, with that particular book, was just one more fulfillment of the promise: "I will also be your light in the wilderness, . . . and ye shall know that it is by me that ye are led (1 Nephi 17:13)" But as I sat in the monitored room, turning the pages of that book with gloved hands, my mind expanded. "Pure design is the composition of tones, measures, shapes, for the sake of rhythm, balance, harmony, the principles of order and beauty."

As I read and learned about these concepts, I found myself desperate to create something. The writing of Claire's story did not completely fill this need as she wasn't really mine. She was a gift.

With Claire's interest in flowers, and her husband's work in design, I decided to redo the landscaping in my front yard and put all of this knowledge to some useful purpose. The area struggled with half-dead quaking aspen that seemed healthier in the spots where they pushed up in the middle of the lawn. An area outside a small wall next to the sidewalk faltered with tangled strawberry plants intertwining thick weeds. We'd had a lot of complaints about the tall stucco wall that surrounded our adjoining lot, which was already there when we moved in. Some of the neighbors weren't shy in telling me it was against code and turned our cul de sac into a prison block.

Work on the yard was intensely physical. We removed and planted everything on our own. Using a rhythm of shapes and layers of different greens, we softened the wall. Keeping in mind the symmetry and harmony of shapes again, we used plants to highlight and balance the architecture of our home. My surroundings improved.

I also considered the yard my living sculpture. Like Claire, I gained meaningful insight as I observed individual patterns of growth and change throughout the seasons. Because I had planted each one, their thriving gave me an added measure of satisfaction. I understood more deeply Claire's love for living things.

Next, I moved to the inside of my home. Mom's wheelchair had damaged my flooring and left marks on the walls. In addition, the house had curtains. How was I supposed to take care of curtains? Kent and I decided to remodel. I spent hours designing. I loved that I could draw what I wanted on paper. I drew my fireplace a hundred times, changing every little detail just to see how it would change the overall effect. I could see what I wanted and what it would look like before we ever started.

Using the concepts of rhythm, balance, and harmony to create order and beauty, we designed and remodeled our home. These changes also had a useful purpose in making our home more functional for our needs.

Once again, the end result was an improvement. There is a part of my soul in this house. As I went through the process, I became acutely aware of the effort it takes to design anything. I had seen my yard before, and after. There was a noticeable improvement. Same with my home. These changes would never have happened on their own. My yard would never have spontaneously rearranged itself into order for the purpose of beautifying my home. The thought of that happening was absurd.

I began taking note of the evidence of design in nature. Something as small and simple as a snail or a seashell, expressed the beauty of perfect proportion known as the infinite curve. Entire books had been written on the beauty of nature's designs, and I have since devoured many of them. The concept that shapes in nature are repeated in different scales captivated me. For example, I was enthralled to learn that in some cases the shape of a leaf is repeated in the shape of the branch, which is then repeated in the shape of the entire plant as a whole. What beautiful designs. Even the human body with its bilateral symmetry and perfect proportions is a study in design. As a tithe payer of ten percent of my income, I was equally fascinated to learn that throughout the food chain, the proportion one rung gives to the next rung up the food chain ladder is consistently ten percent throughout the ecosystem. I discovered that in everything, there is an amazing demonstration of rhythm, balance, and harmony.

The evidence was all around me, and always had been. This world was designed. My body, as imperfect as it happened to be, was designed. The thought that life in all its forms, variety, and complexity could have organized itself out of soup is as implausible to me now as to consider my yard re-landscaping itself into something of purpose or my home remodeling itself into something more useful.

Along with this realization came a desire to know more about the designer. And these things I know: the Designer of this world loves order and beauty. He glories in variety and is attentive to even the smallest detail. He sees color, He smells, He can feel, He tastes, and He experiences joy. He believes in change and seasons. His purpose is growth, replenishment, and renewal.

I now see Him in His works. He is in and through all of them. The same is true for me. I have come to acknowledge that because I am one of His designs, He is also in me.

24

PURPOSES

Near the end of my patriarchal blessing it tells me the Lord has definite purposes in store for me, "Seek to know what these purposes are, and they will be revealed." I share this knowing these words are true for all people, not just for me. But here is the personal part—I have prayed my whole life to know what these purposes are, and they have yet to be fully revealed.

I have, however, followed the light preparing the way before me, wondering where I am being led.

As I continued to write Claire's story, I often read back over what I had written. I rubbed my forehead and pounded my temples. Why couldn't I convey the power of her story? This fictional woman had changed my life for the better, but when I read the events that carried such meaning for me, they seemed ordinary. How could I tell her story with more emotion and power?

Here again, synchronicity played a role. I began reading books on writing. Granted, many of them were ancient and recommended conventions that had dropped out of favor, but while reading the paper one day, I came across a notice for the League of Utah Writer's Workshop. Maybe this would help. I called, not knowing anything about the organization or anyone involved, and signed up. I soon realized how much I didn't know. There were probably 150 people and as I sat at a random table, the group spoke about critique groups, submissions, and contracts. These people were serious writers. Although I could not relate with their experience, I tapped into their passion. The President of the League, Bettyanne, welcomed everyone with confidence and warmth.

I can't remember the specifics of how it happened, but the week after the conference, I found myself sitting at Bettyanne's kitchen table with a group of other writers. For the first time, I began sharing Claire's story.

Every person who has ever attempted to write will relate to this feeling. It's the moment when you step over the threshold and expose your work. It is similar to presenting yourself emotionally naked. Thoughts and stories that have up until now remained private, you set before other critical, expert mothers and ask, "What do you think of my child?"

In a kind and gentle way, this group gave me the feedback I probably already knew but didn't want to hear. I wrote like a novice. As the author, I interrupted the story. I used passive sentences with clunky phrases. Just to make sure the reader understood, I repeated important points with clichéd emphasis. I told Claire's story in a narrative format. The little dialogue I included sounded stilted and unnatural. My story had no shape or flow. I don't think I missed making any possible mistake. Bless these writers. In a figurative way, they put their arms around me and said, "We will help you."

I came home and threw what I had written in the garbage. What was I thinking? I thought I had been given something grand and wonderful, and I had made it trivial. That bothered me the most. For several days, I couldn't face it. I blocked out every thought of writing a word or attempting to tell Claire's story.

But it wouldn't rest. I had to write that story. I thought about the feedback I'd been given and set out to revise my mess.

What a difference a little change made. Each word had power. If I chose the right nouns and verbs and placed them correctly, a few words carried more impact than an entire paragraph. When I read over my revision, the story spoke with more power. I held the page to my chest and thanked those writers for their honesty and help.

Every week I attended my critique group around Bettyanne's kitchen table, thinking my story had reached perfection. I always left disappointed, and it took a day or two to repair my confidence before following their advice. The story inevitably improved.

Those who have been in a critique group are smiling. They know what it's like to hear really bad writing. And they know what it's like to hear the same revised story week after week. I put these patient souls through tremendous pain. Bettyanne took me aside one week and explained, "You know, no matter how many times you revise it, it is still the same story. Move on."

I eventually wrote part of Claire's story into a novel. I submitted this to the League of Utah Writer's competition. It did win first place, but even the judges had reservations about the writing. There were problems with the story's structure. It was a framed story full of flashbacks, which are currently out of fashion. It wasn't fresh and lacked that "larger than life" quality that makes for a good read.

I passed it around to a few good friends and the response was kind, but there were no requests for the sequel. I didn't blame them. It's really tough to slog through bad writing.

Claire resides now in my drawer. I never did finish her full story. For so long I carried her around in my mind, unraveling every detail, certain I wouldn't forget. Later surgeries would wreak havoc on my memory, and almost everything I didn't write down has been lost. I came to realize she would never mean to others what she meant to me. She had served her purpose.

I did move on from Claire's story and began writing other novels and magazine articles. I even came to realize I wasn't going crazy. At different workshops and writers' meetings, other authors talked about my same experience, of having a story come to them, of having characters and their stories presented without asking. I was normal. Maybe I was supposed to be a writer. I dutifully submitted to agents and editors and smiled at my growing pile of rejections. Only about a hundred more and I was bound to be published.

At what would become my last workshop, I submitted three stories to an agent. He met with me, having read what I submitted. He rolled his tongue over his lip and paused.

Was this the break I was waiting for?

"There is an element of sadness to your work." He went on to add several other valid criticisms of my writing.

But those first words, "There is an element of sadness to your work," centered my thoughts and stopped in my heart. We write who we are. The agent knew this. He stared at me as he handed over the file of my work. I stared back as I took it, "Thank you."

I hadn't been aware of this sadness in myself, but in only a few pages, he saw it through my writing. I had some work to do. In some way, I had to purge myself of sadness. For quite a while, I pondered the direction of my life. Claire's story had changed me. It drew me into living again, and I became an interested student of all things human. I would probably never be a great writer. I lacked that natural, intuitive gift, but writing Claire's story had improved my ability. I understood better the power of words. Not only can they describe an experience, they can also give it color and emotion. Words can not only convey our perceptions, opinions, relationships, memories, moods, and feelings, but by selecting words with subtle nuances, we can actually change the perceptions, opinions, relationships, memories, moods and feelings of others. Words have power.

Although I recognized I needed to make some changes in my life and work past the sadness, I continued to attend my critique group. Several of our members became published authors. They accomplished a life-long goal, and I was thrilled for them and their achievement, but it also opened my eyes. Once published, they had to become their own promoter. If they wanted to sell books, they had to generate their own publicity. I had to ask, "Is this my goal? Is this how I want to spend my time? Will this help me become who I need to be?"

One of the women in the group talked about reading *The Artists Way* by Julia Cameron. This author is well-known for helping struggling writers overcome a creative block. I wasn't feeling particularly blocked, but I was intrigued. I began reading her book and started her recommended practice of doing morning pages, writing a stream of consciousness every day along with following her prompts.

I began this on March 5, 2003, with the words, "Today is the first day of my morning pages. I am so excited and have been thinking all night and morning of what I would write—looking forward to putting all my frustrations on paper in order to move on with my life."

Two days later, on March 7, I turned my pages into a prayer.

> Father, thank you for guiding me and revealing yourself to me in the smallest details of my life. I see thee everywhere, and in everything, and I am comforted. I feel your power even now lifting me, surrounding me. I want to do good. I want to be an influence for good in the lives of others. I want to help those who are spiritually wounded. You have all the answers. Thou knowest everything. I know I am weak. Please make me strong. Am I doing what I should? Am I where I should be? I am learning that life is in the details, in the little things, and I am trying harder to do

all the little things. What do you want
me to do? You have given me some
incredible opportunities for growth.
What would thou have me do with these
experiences?

There is a break in my notes, followed by the words:

Lessons God Taught Me. What a
gift this idea is. All I ask is help through
the project to convey thy wisdom and
love throughout the work.

I am stunned. I had forgotten all about that idea I
received five years ago, on the very first day I started my
morning pages, but here I am in the process of trying to do
exactly that.

At that time, my pages affected me in other important
ways. They made me aware of all my negative self-talk. Without
realizing it, I spoke with cruelty to myself. Each day I would
write affirmations and then record my hurtful internal responses.
To my first affirmation—"I am an instrument in God's hand"—I
would respond to myself, "You are unworthy." In overcoming
this blurt, I responded instead, "I am His creation, and He will
help me."

The second day, when I wrote, "God can and will show
me the way," my initial response was, "Who are you to expect
such things from God?" My revised reaction became, "I am His
daughter."

Every day I practiced treating myself kindly, and as I did,
my life once again changed for the better.

This reorientation helped reorganize my thoughts. It
brought into focus what I wanted out of life. I didn't have a
desire to be published; I only wanted to make a difference.
Writing took a huge amount of my time but wasn't leading me
where I wanted to end up. I didn't know exactly what I was

supposed to do, but I knew there was something else. I began praying once again to know what my purposes were and to ask if they could be revealed.

I remember the week I attended my last critique group. By this time, Andrew and Janice were teenagers. I told these women, whom I had grown to love and admire, that I had reevaluated my life goals. Writing novels and magazine articles no longer seemed to fit in with my life's plan. I thanked them for how they had nurtured and encouraged me, but it was time for me to travel in a different direction.

It seems a contradiction. I had learned words have the power to change everything, and I was no longer interested in being published. I didn't understand, but I prayed for direction and enrolled in the preservice training to teach seminary. My neighbor, Stephanie, also showed up the first day of class.

I have reread my patriarchal blessing. It mentions only two gifts I have specifically been given: The gift of the Holy Ghost and the gift of communication. I am still praying to know what definite purposes the Lord has in store for me. I am now forty-eight, and they have yet to be revealed.

25

MOLDING

I need to take a step backwards. My interest in writing spanned nearly a decade, and though it was a hobby, it was not my focus. My family was my life. Up until now I have not written much about Janice and Andrew growing up, mostly because I have tried to concentrate on the singular experiences that affected my relationship with God. The challenge of writing this kind of record is giving an accurate reflection of my life as a whole. Whatever I spend the most time writing about will naturally slant a perception of me in that direction.

So it was with my preoccupation with Claire's life. Though her story elevated my thoughts, gave me new interests, and enriched my life, I still woke up every morning and spent my day caring for my family. I was so grateful I could. One of my biggest mistakes as a mother was not expecting my kids to contribute more. I loved that I could do things for them, since my Mom never could for me. And knowing that one day my family might have to take care of me, I wanted to make huge deposits in my service account. Maybe if I nurtured them with love, they would return the favor in my time of need.

MOLDING

When Janice was about eight and Andrew six, Kent's life-long dream of owning mules became a reality. It's a long story completely beyond my purpose, but these new "pets" Kent kept in Cedar Fort provided a wonderful opportunity for the kids to learn how to work. They also gave an excuse for our family to spend time together.

At one point when I was helping Kent dig post holes and string barbed wire and the kids were dutifully clearing away rocks, I leaned back on my heels and thought, *Whoa. I could never have imagined myself doing this.*

Let's be honest, mules are not your average hobby.

But Janice loved the mules. She had a small black mule named Rose who was so gentle, and Janice seemed to enjoy being with Rose more than she liked being with kids her own age. Janice was a strong-willed child with a big personality. She sucked her thumb into elementary school and no one dared tease her because she would tease them back. I would often try and temper her responses, but she would tell me, "You always say, 'Treat others the way you want to be treated,' Mom, and if they're teasing me, then they want to be teased back."

She had strong opinions and was not afraid to share them. I often looked at her wondering, *Is this the child I felt so strongly had the gift of love for other people?* In private I'd scold her, "That tongue of yours is like a wild horse, rein it in."

Janice and I struggled in our relationship. She didn't like the way I did her hair or the shoes I wanted her to wear. Imagine that. One day after watching the two of us argue, Kent took me aside and asked, "Who is the child here?"

Janice was so bright, she was always four steps ahead of me. She knew the quickest and easiest methods of pushing all my buttons until I responded emotionally. Some mornings I would send her out the door to school and think, *How is she going to make it through this day with a beginning like that?*

Oftentimes, I was still trembling from a disagreement, but I would sit on my front room couch and close my eyes. I would imagine the Savior putting His arm around her and

159

walking her to school. I would imagine her hugging Him back before walking through her class door. "What am I supposed to do with this child?" I would ask. The answer was always the same, "Love her."

On a particularly contentious day, in answer to my frustration, I received the strongest impression. The same qualities that made her so difficult to live with were the same ones Janice would need to accomplish her life mission.

This new insight did nothing to change Janice, but it affected me. I stopped trying to change her into me. I recognized she was a different person, living in different times, with a different purpose to perform. I stood corrected.

With my altered attitude, we grew closer, confirming I had been the problem all along. As she entered junior high school, I was still concerned that instead of being outgoing, active, and interested, she became more sedentary, choosing to sit alone in her darkened room. A pain showed through her eyes.

Then came the events of 9/11. Without saying anything, we all braced for change, not knowing what shape it would take. My concerns about Janice seemed a little smaller.

It was the holiday season of 2001, and the city was preparing to host the Salt Lake City Winter Olympics in February of 2002. Mitt Romney had recharged the community with enthusiasm after the Olympic bid scandal left us embarrassed and ashamed.

For years we had read the papers and watched the news about yet another dignitary's visit to the state as we hoped to win the Olympic bid. The VIP in the attending picture always held a souvenir. We knew they were being given gifts but were sad to learn many had taken the form of bribes. I don't think, however, that many of us were surprised.

I was grateful when the truth came out. I could just imagine some worker in the Olympic office with a conscience who was sickened by the process. The story actually broke on our local news. Though there was some comfort in admitting our own guilt, the worldwide aftermath left us feeling bruised.

Mitt Romney changed all that. I am no expert, but it seemed he did it through his positive momentum and organization. The moment he stepped in, the vague became detailed. Every concern was addressed with a workable solution. Security issues, since 9/11 had only happened a few months earlier, required new and unique approaches. No problem. Every scenario was considered and measures were put in place to protect the world in our city. When Mitt Romney would later run for the presidency in the 2008 election, his 90 percent win in Utah was mischaracterized by the national press as a "Mormon vote." There aren't enough Mormons to achieve that number. It was a vote of recognition and thanks for something magnificent that impacted each one of us for the better.

The whole city was excited to be a part of something so much bigger than ourselves. Many in my neighborhood volunteered and were in the process of attending various training sessions. I had been to several already.

I was taking Janice in for her routine screening. Given her 50 percent genetic possibility for VHL, I had her eyes checked every year for any evidence of the disease. Tumors in the retina had been my first symptom. I had several things planned after her appointment.

The doctor took one look and sat back. He took in a deep breath and looked at me. "I don't want to have to tell you this."

He didn't need to say anymore. The room remained silent for a moment. I looked at Janice and she was no longer so different from me.

Our lives change so fast sometimes. It only takes ten words or less. I didn't cry. Neither did she. We finished the appointment and walked to the car.

"I'm sorry," I told her.

"It's okay, Mom," she answered.

In my mind I churned out details. Get the tumors treated with laser, call and get an MRI of the brain ordered.

"Let's have a plan," I told her. "Let's make sure we have all our tests done each year, and then let's not think about this disease unless we have to." I held my thumb and index finger close until they were almost touching. "Let's only let this disease have this much of our lives."

She hinted a smile. "Deal."

I called my neurosurgeon and he ordered an MRI of her brain. When he called to tell me she had a tumor, my whole body went numb. When I told Kent, he clenched his jaw. "Let's get her the best pediatric neurosurgeon we can find."

He started calling his cardiologists and asking for referrals. When the majority of them recommended the same doctor, we called and made an appointment. He could see us the week before Christmas.

I felt as though I had taken in a deep breath at the eye doctor's and still hadn't been able to exhale. A storm hovered over the holidays. The approaching Olympics and 9/11 retreated. I attended one more volunteer training session unsure if I would be available.

When I sat down on Janice's bed to tell her about the brain tumor, I looked into her eyes. They had shown pain for a while now, but with the bad news, she seemed relieved. Though she had never mentioned a word or complained, she now admitted she had been having headaches and that bright lights bothered her eyes.

When we met with the neurosurgeon, he confirmed the presence of a tumor in the cerebellum. More troubling than the tumor was the swelling. It needed to come out. We scheduled the surgery for January 18, 2002. We wanted to have her home before the city became a security zone with the Olympics in February, especially since the athlete's village was situated next to the hospital. I withdrew from my Olympic volunteer assignment.

The time between our appointment and the surgery inched along. I could not hold on to peace and felt my confidence in the outcome slipping every day. By the time we were a day or two out, I was an emotional *Titanic.* Kent was as well. I attended the temple and quietly sobbed through the entire ceremony. Janice on the other hand, seemed very calm. She did, however, begin running a fever that went as high as 104. She was diagnosed with strep and started on antibiotics.

The night before her surgery, Kent could not give Janice a priesthood blessing. He was too anxious to be open and objective. Instead, he asked his father, Janice's grandfather, to come over and give it. Before Ralph even started, I was already crying. I wanted peace. I didn't want her surgery delayed because of her strep infection. I wanted to hear the surgery would go okay and she would recover and have all of her functions. That's it. That's all I wanted.

In my journal of that day, I wrote the things I could remember from that blessing. Ralph blessed Janice that she would be healed of her infirmity. Her surgery would not be delayed. Her surgeons and caregivers would be blessed and guided. This was all I had wanted, but Ralph continued. As he spoke, I wanted to lift my head and open my eyes. He unfolded Janice's life and the significant role she would play in furthering God's work here on the earth.

I kept thinking, "This is Janice? My Janice?"

When the blessing was over, I opened my eyes and saw a new child. She was only thirteen, and at such a young age, carried a large responsibility. To accomplish the great work she would be asked to do, she would need experiences to prepare her. This disease and surgery were all part of that preparation. God would protect her. I could entrust her into His care.

The surgery did go well. She was back in school a month later. With the tumor gone, we noticed a drastic change for the better in her personality. The pain was gone and so was her desire for solitude in a darkened room. Almost immediately, she came to life. Her gift of love made its debut as she reached out to others with friendship and compassion.

I know I'm seeing her through a mother's eye, but we witnessed a beautiful transformation in her spirit and attitude. Given that she was thirteen and just starting into the "terrible teens," we couldn't have been more grateful.

I have included Janice's story in my record because I think of all I have been through in my life, this was by far the most difficult. Years before, when Janice and Andrew were little, I returned to my eye doctor in San Francisco for a checkup. I had not seen him in many years and when he found out I had children, he shook his head. "How could you have children when you know you might be passing this disease on?"

He was right. I knew. At that time, we didn't know if either of the kids had it. I dreaded thinking they might. And for all that I had been through, I couldn't blame my mom, because she didn't know she had the disease, but I did.

I remember after the doctor asked me that question, looking directly into his eyes and answering, "That's why I could never have made this decision alone. I don't know enough to make such an important decision. I had to rely on someone who knows all things from the beginning to the end to make that decision for me. In answer to your question, I did not make this decision alone."

He accepted my answer without argument.

I did have help in my decision as to whether or not I should have children, but it was still my decision. And I accept full responsibility for the outcome. I do not deserve any special treatment, and I am not entitled to any special blessings, but in my heart is a prayer that God will heal her. I pray this disease will rest lightly on her shoulders. And like my mom, if there is anything I can go through or suffer so she won't have to, I am happy to do so.

To her credit, Janice has never expressed any anger or resentment toward me for her illness. She rarely speaks of it at all to anyone. She simply hefts her cumbersome burden on her way forward through life. Her view from under that weight gives her a little different perspective. I believe this new vision is a gift. It is a source of inner strength and maturity that will guide her to do great things with her life.

I look forward to reading Janice's story one day and how she perceived these same events. Though it is frightening, and I will feel responsible for every challenge she faces with this disease, I am also thrilled to have a front row seat to the unfolding of her destiny. I both dread and rejoice at how God will maneuver her opportunities in order for her to accomplish her earthly mission.

26

ACKNOWLEDGING GLORY

I am happy to say it did not always take a difficult trial or tragic event for me to discover a great truth about my relationship with God. Some things I actually figured out on my own. One night Kent and I went out to dinner with some dear friends. This couple did not share our religious beliefs, so religion was not generally a topic for discussion. I don't know how it came up, but the husband commented that if God existed, He would have to "make Himself known" personally to him.

I respected our friend's opinion and right to believe the way he wished, but as the conversation of the evening continued, he mentioned some amazing occurrences that had taken place in his life. One of his children had experienced a miraculous transformation. Where before his daughter had been devastated by addictions and personal problems, she had discovered religion and turned her life around. Our friend had also been through a financial crisis that had largely resolved itself. The list of what he would have called lucky events went on and on.

When we arrived home, I couldn't stop thinking about our friend's expectation that God would have to declare Himself in order for our friend to believe. I wondered what form God would have to take?

I turned in the New Testament to the story of the scribes and the Pharisees asking the Savior for a sign of His divinity (see Matthew 12:38). I caught something I had never noticed before. Just prior to their asking for a sign, the scriptures say, "Great multitudes followed [Jesus Christ], and he healed them all" (v. 15). What more could the Savior have done to convince the scribes and Pharisees? What exactly were they looking for? Jesus described their inability to believe on Him by saying, "They seeing see not; and hearing they hear not, neither do they understand" (Matthew 13:13).

In a beautiful moment of enlightenment, I realized God is continually making himself known to us. How much of it do we miss? How much was I missing? Since I was writing my morning pages anyway, I decided to make a review every day of the moments when God made Himself known to me. I noted answered prayers, small coincidences, events when things worked out to my benefit, chance meetings, and opportunities that came my way. A beautiful thing happened. These moments began happening more frequently.

Because I am the way I am, I had to analyze this. Were they really happening more frequently, or was I just getting better at noticing them? After several days, I had to admit, good things happened more often in my life.

There was a principle here I wanted to understand. My life had been blessed simply by acknowledging the times when God helped me. Why? How did it work? I came across several scriptures. The first was D&C 59:21: "And in nothing doth man offend God, or against none is his wrath kindled, save those who confess not his hand in all things, and obey not his commandments." This might not seem helpful, but when I turned it around, I discovered something amazing: "And in nothing doth man please God, or is his peace kindled, save those who confess his hand in all things, and obey his commandments."

Then I found this one, D&C 71:6: "For unto him that receiveth it shall be given more abundantly, even power." By simply acknowledging God's power in my life, I was in fact "receiving" Him and what He was offering. By so doing, He was in fact giving me more abundantly. It was true. Just to confirm this, I found another, D&C 78:19: "And he who receiveth all things with thankfulness shall be made glorious; and the things of this earth shall be added unto him, even an hundred fold, yea, more."

It is my privilege to include this principle in my life story. I want to acknowledge to one and all, my gratitude for all the good that has come to me in my life. Some of the most beautiful of these moments have been the smallest. It is when God makes himself known to me in the littlest of details that I know He is aware and concerned about everything in my life. He is glorious and generous and I am oh so grateful.

27

MY TURN

My neurosurgeon had been following the brain tumors for years, but now one had developed a cyst. The time had come for three of them to be removed. I say "three" because they were close enough to be removed at the same time, but there was another one too far away to be included in this operation. If I was lucky, it wouldn't grow and I would never have to have it out.

This must sound crazy to healthy people, but I was relieved at the prospect of having brain surgery. For several years, I had noticed the light of life dimming. Since the combined tumor growth had been small and incremental, my brain had accommodated the change fairly well, but over several years, their size eventually had an impact. Add to this now a cyst, which grew much faster than the tumors combined, and I could feel myself changing.

Everything irritated me. My arms and fingers must have shortened as I felt distanced from the physical world. I couldn't seem to reach others, and there was interference in our connection. The colors and hues of living diminished. I became easily fatigued and lacked motivation. Worst of all, I said the stupidest, hurtful things. I didn't mean to. I think it stemmed from the fact that I was not feeling well, and in my disengaged state of mind, projected my own misery on to everyone around me.

Here is one example. I had agreed to help with Janice's sixth-grade Valentine's dance at the school gymnasium. At the party were the parents of one of her friends who had also agreed to help. One of the mothers had lost quite a bit of weight. Rather than being pleasant and telling her she looked great, I said, (and I cringe in admitting this,) "Have you been sick? Are you feeling well? Is everything going okay?"

The only reason I am including this is because I honestly don't know how many people I offended during this time of my life. For all those I insulted, I hope they will one day understand that I didn't intend to say anything unkind or mean and that my comments resulted from my not feeling well. I ask their forgiveness.

Without beating the life out of this issue, I had a vague sense of detachment, but I don't think I realized how much the tumors were affecting me until after I had them out.

The surgery went fine. Before the orderly rolled me into the operating room on the stretcher, I said to my neurosurgeon, "I've told everyone I'm coming in for a brain augmentation. They're going to be really disappointed if I don't come out speaking Spanish fluently."

His eyes opened wide, "Uh, maybe we need to talk about exactly what we're doing in there."

"It's okay if I don't speak Spanish," I told him. "Just take good care of my brain."

"That I can do," he told me, giving me a smile and a pat on my shoulder.

And he did. My surgery was on October 20, 2002. I was home three days later. Though I felt as though my one head was the size of two, the recovery was not so bad. Since not too many muscles had been cut, I could get up and move around. I could eat normally and actually felt better sitting up. The only glitch in the whole brain surgery was when the resident told me to come in and have my staples removed too early. I didn't figure this out until the staples were already gone and my incision separated. It took three months to finally heal, but there weren't any complications other than a really ugly incision under my hair. One of the most joyful experiences was lying on my back again. Any previously pregnant woman will appreciate how wonderful that felt.

It took some time, but I felt as though I had reentered the world. Little things gave me the greatest joy. Andrew had just started taking art classes and he was seeing the world differently too. We became fellow admirers of all things unique and beautiful. "Mom, come see the clouds," he would say, leading me outside to look at the sky. Andrew was twelve years old at the time.

He became my "sunset buddy." Since the western sky is behind our neighbors' homes, Andrew would go with me through the school walkway to Antczak Park where we would climb the ladder to the top of the school playground slide and watch the lowering of the sun into the horizon with all its color and glory. We both sighed as that beautiful globe of light gave one last exclamation of day before descending below the earth's horizon. I enjoyed it all the more because Andrew was with me.

I love this world and confess I am partial to its sky. I look forward to opening my blinds every morning and meeting the new day. Is it going to be clear or overcast? Whenever I'm outside, I study the clouds. Before digital cameras, I had rolls of film with nothing but sky in the picture. You can just imagine what my home movies are like. We went to visit some friends who had a beautiful home overlooking the Ogden Valley. Large picture windows opened the view from every angle. They couldn't pull me away. I wasn't even looking at the city; I was watching a storm with angry, seething clouds crawling by.

I celebrate every season, but fall is my favorite. My digital picture cards are full of colored leaves. Those vibrant, autumn oranges take my breath away. They blaze for such a spectacularly short time. Spring is my next favorite with the green lawns and snow-capped mountains against the backdrop of a brilliant, blue sky.

My religious doctrine teaches me I'm here on earth because I needed to have a body. Imperfect as mine might be, I'm taught I cannot experience a fullness of joy without it. Now, isn't that ironic? I have always thought it quite profound that God's creation of the world concluded not in dirt and water, but in human form, male and female. Of all the beauty and magnificence around us, we are his most beloved and precious creations.

Maybe it's because marriage has been so prominent in the news lately that questions about its significance and meaning have sprinkled over my brain and filtered down through my heart and into my soul. Throw in my life's experiences, this incredible world, my physical challenges, along with the society we live in, and a new perception has risen to the surface.

We are all a metaphor of marriage.

Each one of us is the creation of something new and living from the joining of our father and our mother. They are both represented equally within us in every single cell. We are their perfect union. We are their marriage.

I marvel that there is a part of me that has lived through every moment of human history, being passed down from generation to generation. My parents were the keepers of a portion of this knowledge that was passed on to them, and now they have passed a new share on to me. There is great power in these traits my parents have given me genetically, but perhaps the greater strength is the wisdom gained and understood from seeing how these traits expressed themselves in them. Despite all their shortcomings and weaknesses, in seeing how my parents overcame the challenges of their day, I learn what is inside of me and what I should or shouldn't do to overcome the obstacles I may face.

Perhaps I am most sensitive to this because I lost my father when I was so young. I miss that part of knowing him and how I was like him. I miss not knowing what is inside of me and makes up half of who I am. In my tapestry of humanity, there is a hole.

With so many questions and new definitions of marriage and family, I realize now how fortunate I was to belong to the father and mother who gave me life, and to have been treasured by the fathers and mothers who gave them their lives. How lucky for me that I've had the chance to then observe and cherish every other man and woman resulting from these relationships. In my own family is a wealth of knowledge about myself, which I had taken completely for granted.

Let me return to my experiences of feeling detached from the world and the people in it prior to my brain surgery. I didn't realize how intricately I was engaged and connected to the world until I became detached. How could I have known? But how fortunate I am to know this now, while I am still alive and can appreciate what it feels like when I am immersed in living again. In this same way, I now recognize every momentary loss I've experienced is a gift.

My mother was also a gift. Given all the trauma to her brain caused by her tumors, radiation, and surgery, she couldn't help being distant and detached. I understand that now, but it took my own brain tumors and more than half a lifetime for me to figure it out. Her losses were also my teachers. Through my experiences caring for her, I learned to appreciate every day the blessing of being able to walk or have the use of my hands. How fortunate I have been to be able to take care of my own personal needs, care for my family, or even complete unpleasant chores. Even though I had to go through brain surgery, I came out okay. I felt better and I could function. I only realized how lucky I was because of Mom's losses. Her life had given me a context for my own.

I often asked the Lord, "Isn't there some other way to learn all of these lessons without having to go through so many trials?"

The answer I received was profound and far beyond my own intelligence to figure out. A whisper spoke to my heart that if I would help bear other's burdens, I could learn those lessons without having to go through them myself. How grateful I am now that I was able to care for my mother. To care for that woman who gave me life and held so many secrets of who I am, who allowed me to bear her burdens so that, hopefully, I won't need to bear those same ones. The Lord commanded, "Honour thy father and thy mother: that thy days may be long upon the land which the Lord thy God giveth thee" (Exodus 20:12). This makes sense to me now. My father and mother have greatly honored me, and I also honor them.

This body they gave me is intended to bring a fulness of joy. How sad that I might not fully appreciate its deep significance until I am separated from it at death. I sometimes wonder what I will miss the most about not having a body. I do know that at some point it will be restored again in its perfect form. I can already sense that when that day comes, I will receive this body back with a fulness of joy at having it returned.

I also realize how much I want to pass on to my own posterity who I am so they will know who they are. Perhaps if I write down my story, it will be my way of sharing my burdens with them, even after I'm gone, and they won't have to experience these same trials. This is certainly my prayer and my wish for them.

28

ALL THINGS SHALL WORK TOGETHER FOR YOUR GOOD

I mentioned much earlier that a neighbor Stephanie and I ended up taking a seminary teaching course together. We actually started September of 2003. I knew I would not be able to become a full-time seminary teacher since I still had minor children living at home. Stephanie, on the other hand, was much closer to having her youngest on his way. He was beginning his senior year in high school as we began the course. At this time, I put aside all my desires to write and though I knew I could not be a regular seminary teacher, I wanted to focus on becoming a better teacher.

Though I tried to leave it alone, writing was in my blood, coursing with a passion I could not easily ignore. I continued my morning pages and recorded not even three weeks into my course a conversation I had with another dear neighbor Diane S. (She is, incidentally, the woman who bought the home I loved when Kent and I were looking to buy one of our own. And I'm so glad she did!) I mentioned to Diane I would love to get a group of writers started in the ward, our local unit of the Church.

Later that day, Diane dropped by with a book I was interested in reading along with a note, "I'm nervous/excited about our possible writing group and need all the help I can get." At that time, I called several other ladies in the neighborhood to see if they had any interest in participating. I shocked myself. I am not the organizing type. I hate being in charge of stuff.

Though our writing group did not take off at that time, I was given a reminder about how these things sometimes have to simmer for a while. An article I submitted years before was finally published in a children's magazine.

About this time, I also ended up in the hospital with pneumonia. I had been having abdominal pain for about a year. A CT scan months earlier didn't show any problems, so I ignored the pain. I slowly accommodated by not breathing too deeply. By the time I went to the doctor, I was almost dead. Didn't it seem I'd had enough medical visits already? At least the majority of my VHL problems were planned in advance and conveniently scheduled.

While in the hospital with pneumonia, I had an unusual physical experience. For several hours my entire body felt as though it were vibrating. I reached out to touch things just to see if my finger was indeed shaking. It wasn't. I placed my vibrating hands around a glass of water, and the water stood still. I have no idea what neurological event was happening, but I could only describe it as a feeling that my spirit was trying to wrench free.

My daily writings after this experience took on a more reflective tone. Was I prepared to leave this world? I considered my life as a whole built on a trellis of tragedy. Yet it was through this framework of despair that I had come to know God. He had revealed Himself to me, covering a bitter lattice with sweet and beautiful mercies. My challenges had been my greatest teachers. They were blessings in my life—gifts of the trellis. The impression came that I needed to record my story. My life had been preserved for this reason. These thoughts fit in well with the seminary theme for that year, "Search diligently, pray always, and be believing, and all things shall work together for your good" (D&C 90:24).

After I recovered, over the next several months, I gently suggested the thought of a writing group to more women. I now presented it as an opportunity to write our personal histories. I knew Stephanie was on board. She had been part of my previous critique group and was such a gifted writer, she could make a sunny day compelling. I patiently waited for this idea to take on a life of its own.

On February 11, 2004, I recorded, "Tomorrow I start this writing group with women in our ward. Tomorrow will be the beginning of something wonderful. I get the feeling this will not be the only group." Even then I had a sense of the importance this group would have in my life.

On March 3, 2004, I came home from my seminary training to ten messages on my answering machine. I never get ten messages in an entire week. Nine of them were from one of Kent's accounts in Montana, the last one was from my neighbor Paul, asking me to call him immediately.

When I called Paul, he told me he was coming right over. He met me at the door and sat me down in the front room. Kent had called him just as he was going into surgery. Everything was fine, but he had been in a head-on car collision in Kalispell, Montana. Kent broke the bones in his lower right arm and was in surgery getting them repaired. As I returned the other nine messages, the situation became clear. It wasn't Kent's fault, (one of my biggest concerns since I know how Kent drives), but he had been hit on a two-lane road. His air bag deployed and broke his arm. When Kent came out of surgery, he called, "Don't come up. I'm fine. It will cost too much money."

I might not have mentioned Kent is tight. He once told me that for him, spending money is like having a baby—very painful. So, every time I write a check, I let him know he's having a contraction. On this occasion, I didn't care how much it cost, he needed help getting home.

I flew up the next morning and one of the nurses from the hospital cath lab picked me up. I was impressed by her detailed description of how Kent was doing. I felt slightly guilty. She and the other cath lab employees were taking better care of him than I would have. No wonder he didn't want me to come. They treated him as if he were a celebrity. One of the doctors even offered to let me stay at his home.

All those years I had felt sorry that Kent had to travel so much. Now I realized he had another loving family in each one of his accounts. We were treated like dignitaries and received far more attention than we deserved.

I was anxious to see Kent for the first time. I didn't know what to expect, given the violence of his collision, but when I saw him, I was shocked there wasn't a mark on his face. He had a scab where his seatbelt held him on his waist, and his right arm was bruised all the way to his armpit. His fingers looked dead—all white and clammy with hardly any color in his nails. But he was fine. He was alive.

This was the first time for me to be in the supportive position in a medical situation. Usually, Kent was the one taking care of me. I appreciated deeply every act of kindness done for Kent. It meant more than I could have imagined.

We left the hospital the next day and flew back to Salt Lake. Partly because of the pain, and partly because of his nursing knowledge about swelling, Kent kept his arm elevated high above his head. Wherever we went, he looked as though he had something to say and was waiting for someone to call on him. We sat down in the plane with his arm raised and the flight attendants kept asking, "Do you need something?" He kept his arm elevated like this for the next eight weeks, even when he slept.

Kent suffered more from not being able to work than from the pain or discomfort from his arm. For the eleven years Kent had been with this company, we had never taken a vacation outside his territory. He had never taken more than seven days off at a time. When the doctor told him he couldn't do anything with the arm for eight weeks, he nearly stopped breathing. "What will happen to my job?" he asked me.

I shook my head. "I don't know. All I know is that if we search diligently, pray always, and be believing, all things will work together for our good." I'm not sure if it was the answer he wanted.

I accompanied Kent on a business trip shortly after his car accident and surgery. He couldn't lift any of his bags, and since his work is mostly on commission and he feared for his job, he asked me to go with him. But when his company found out, they banned him from any trips until he had been released by the doctor. That nearly drove him crazy with worry. What would happen to his job? Would his customers stick with his products? Would the competition, knowing about his accident, move in and take over his accounts?

All I could say was, "Search diligently, pray always, and be believing, and all things will work together for your good."

I came to realize several things. Kent makes great sacrifices for our family. His greatest worry in life is taking care of us. He carries this responsibility with him twenty-four hours a day, seven days a week. I realized how lucky I am he is willing to shoulder this burden. As much as I hate having health issues, I'm grateful it's me and not him. Because he is willing to solely provide for our family, the impact of my recoveries is less complicated for the family.

The selfish part of me loved having this eight-week time period with Kent. I was grateful for the chance to return the favor and take care of him. And during this time, I sought diligently, prayed always, and believed that things would work together for our good.

Every day I recorded the wonderful gifts that came our way. I made myself a note that I would receive with thankfulness all God had to offer me. I came to recognize His assurance that all things would work together for our good was the greatest of all the gifts I received.

A month after Kent went back to work, the company announced changes in the compensation package. It wasn't a good change for our family and meant less pay. While we were figuring out how this would affect us, his boss called. Each manager had been allowed to choose two reps to include on a retention plan, guaranteeing their income. His manager had chosen Kent as one of his two.

I know Kent appreciates his job. He's a hard worker, and he's good at what he does, but the other reps in Kent's region are also talented and devoted employees. Our individual efforts must seem so puny to God, the creator of the world, who has all power and knows all things. Kent knew where this mercy regarding his job came from. I love him all the more for that.

29

LEARNING TO LISTEN

On August 4, 2004, I had a checkup with my neuro-surgeon. The whole time I waited to see him in the clinic, I felt sick to my stomach. A huge dark cloud hung over me, and I felt irritable. It was a Wednesday.

For some time prior, I had been contemplating my relationship with the Savior. I believe I knew Him before I came to this world. I believe I knew He would atone for my sins and weaknesses, and that's why I chose to come. I believe I had a choice. I didn't have to be born, and no one made me. I chose to be here.

The Savior is my only explanation for why I didn't stay in that pre-earthly realm. I must have loved Him. I must have trusted Him. I must have known He would find me. I thank Him for finding me. And just as it was a choice for me to be here, I believe He wants to be a choice here on this earth as well. He honors choice.

I stopped searching for "the undisputable proof" that Jesus Christ is the Son of God, the Messiah and Redeemer of all mankind. For every claim He makes, unbelievers will always come up with a viable alternative. It's their choice to do so, and I honor their right to make it. The Savior honors it as well. He gave it to them. I believe that's what His sacrifice was all about. Choice.

As I sat in that doctor's office, feeling sick and awful, waiting to hear about the status of my tumors, I whispered to my Savior. "I choose You. No matter what happens, I choose to believe in You."

The tumor in my brain also had a cyst. It had grown. Within the year, I would need another brain surgery.

I'm normal. For the next several weeks my mortal mind argued, "If you believe in God, why does He allow you to suffer? If He has all power, why doesn't He help you? He can take this away, why doesn't He do it?"

John the Baptist entered my thoughts. A strange connection perhaps, but in my mind, I imagined him there in Herod's jail. On several occasions, he had borne witness of the Savior. The first time came before he was even born as he leaped in his mother's womb at the sound of Mary's voice (see Luke 1:40-44). He also testified as he baptized in the river Jordan, "There cometh one mightier than I after me, the latchet of whose shoes I am not worthy to stoop down and unloose. I indeed have baptized you with water: but he shall baptize you with the Holy Ghost" (Mark 1:7-8). John also received incredible witnesses. After baptizing the Savior, He saw the heavens open, and the Spirit like a dove descending. He heard the Voice of Heaven declare of Christ, "Thou art my beloved Son; in thee I am well pleased" (Luke 3:21-22).

But there John the Baptist sat in Herod's prison, anticipating his fate. The scriptures don't say exactly when John sent his disciples to ask the Savior, "Art thou he that should come? or look we for another?" (Luke 7:19-20) but I would imagine it was about this time. If the Savior could perform miracles on behalf of God, he could certainly help John, couldn't he? After all, John the Baptist was a righteous man. The Savior said so himself. He described John as "more than a prophet. For this is he, of whom it is written, Behold, I send my messenger before thy face, which shall prepare thy way before thee" (Matthew 11:9-10).

But Jesus Christ did not save John.

The scriptures do not tell us anything about how John the Baptist reconciled this. Wise and learned men have suggested the reason John sent his disciples to Christ was so these followers would know for themselves and receive their own testimony of the Savior, since John knew he was going to die. His faith in the Savior never wavered. I cannot argue or dispute this interpretation.

At that time in my life, however, I projected my own questions and doubts on to John. Maybe he wondered why the Savior would heal and bless so many others, when he, John, had been a devoted servant, and he received no miracle, no deliverance, no intervention. I ached for this John of my imagination and pondered how or if he resolved this dilemma.

Two distinct impressions came. First, if John had a question, he took his concern directly to the Savior. He didn't seek other opinions, and he didn't vent his frustrations to anyone else other than the Savior Himself. John trusted and loved Him that much.

Secondly, John's mission was to prepare the way before the Savior. He did this in life and would now perform this great service also in death. Did John know his death served a grand purpose? I wondered. I suspect at some point he did, and I suspect he considered it a privilege.

This one grabbed me. It took me by the collar, stood me up a little taller, and seemed to ask, "Do you understand what this means?" Figuratively, I nodded. The Savior would not take away John's mission.

It was not long before the Savior himself asked for intervention in Gethsemane, "O my Father, if it be possible, let this cup pass from me" (Matthew 26:39).

I took in a deep breath. Christ had a destiny. My eternal life depended on His success. God would not take that away from Him. I believe John knew this as well.

I love John the Baptist. He is one of my heroes. I decided to follow his example and prayed to know, "God, do you love me? Are you who you claim to be? If not, then where should I turn for help?"

Then I listened. And I waited for Him to answer. Almost a month later, I received an answer. "Thou art blessed. I am near thee. I shall make up any difference. Be humble and I will lead thee. Thy children shall do great works. Be patient, be kind, be loving, be encouraging, be forgiving. Move forward. I will guide thee. I will enlighten thee. It is time to write. Use your time wisely. Care for the needs of others. Be thoughtful. Be concerned. Don't be afraid to help. Don't be afraid to offer."

I was overwhelmed with His kindness and the gentleness of His words. From that day forward, I listened. As I contemplated the reality of another brain surgery, I was encouraged to "Look forward to the future. Thy greatest days are yet to come."

I know what they'll say. Unbelievers will read my story and shout, "This woman had an active brain tumor. Hello. This is a classic example of temporal-lobe personality, possibly caused by temporal-lobe epilepsy (TLE.) The literature is full of people like her with similar experiences."

People who suffer from TLE have seizures in the temporal lobe region of the brain. This condition can occur as a result of an infection, a genetic predisposition, or from something such as a tumor. In some cases (and I emphasize SOME), individuals with TLE are described as having hypergraphia (excessive writing,) a sense of personal destiny, as being overly moral, as well as deeply religious. There have been a few cases where TLE patients claim to have profound spiritual experiences.

My tumors, actually, have all been in the cerebellum. That's not to say a tumor with a cyst there could not create pressure in other areas of my brain. But to my knowledge, I have never had a seizure. Regardless, I know there will be those who present this as THE explanation for my experiences.

As I mentioned before, believing in God is a choice. I present my impressions, my thoughts, my feelings, and let you decide for yourself. I have already made my decision.

About this time, Janice complained of difficulty eating. She often coughed, and it was taking longer to get her food down. An MRI confirmed a small tumor in her brain stem, near the nerve affecting her ability to swallow. A swallow test confirmed certain foods, such as peanut butter, were difficult to clear. Janice asked me, "Mom, why can't I just have this tumor out?" I agreed. I called the neurosurgeon, and he confided he was worried surgery might leave Janice with a permanent tracheotomy. It was a fine line. If her problems with swallowing got worse and she began aspirating food into the lungs, she'd need a tracheotomy anyway. The tumor might not grow for many years. It was best to wait and watch.

At this time, she was also having problems with her vision. A tumor on her optic nerve was leaking fluid. Normally, tumors in the retina are treated with laser surgery, but with the tumor directly on the nerve, this was not an option. There were in fact no options. As Janice's vision continued to deteriorate, under the doctor's recommendation, we decided to try mild laser treatments to parts of the tumor furthest away from the nerve. It didn't work. Fluid continued to leak, and the scar tissue pulled everything out of whack. Janice was left with double-vision and an active tumor.

I prayed. What was I supposed to do? So many big things were happening, I needed answers. As I listened, here was my reply: "Be not afraid, for I am with thee. Treasure up these experiences—they shall be tender, marvelous memories, and the strength and wisdom gained will be of benefit to many. All will be well. Search diligently, pray always, and be believing, and all things, including these things, shall work for your good. Janice is being prepared for great things."

Words do not allow me to express the comfort I received from this message. I confess, however, that I was a little unnerved by the process. Was God really talking so directly to

185

me, or was this my hopeful imagination? My life was in chaos. These words were calm and reassuring. Could I really trust that everything would be okay?

By Halloween of that year, I constantly had a lump in my throat from my worry and distress over Janice. This didn't do much to help my own brain tumor. Reassurances continued to come, "Be thou still and know that I am God. Peace be unto thy soul for I am with thee and will bear thee up. Stay close to me and every need shall be met. Janice shall grow stronger. This experience will give her strength. It will increase her influence with those around her. She will be a source of inspiration to all who know her. Through this experience, she will gain the power to lift others. She will gain the strength to bear other's burdens and guide them safely through. She will gain the faith necessary to perform mighty works among her peers."

I heard these words in my mind and clearly felt them in my heart. Why was it so hard for me to trust in them? When I had these beautiful assurances, why did I still worry? But I did. My emotions remained on edge and I found myself weeping at odd times for no apparent reason. I know this was tumor related, but my lack of control over my own emotions added to my frustration.

One late evening when I was walking down the hall in our home, I overheard Janice talking on the phone to a friend who was having a hard time dealing with life in general. After a time of quiet listening, Janice responded, "I have no problems. The ones I have are so small."

I think I wept that whole night. I don't believe she ever told any of her friends at that time what she was going through.

One of the great blessings I received during this time was a new backyard. Nanny (my mother's mother) passed away, and we had been told she would be leaving her estate to her surviving children. Since our mother preceded her in death, we did not expect to receive anything. As it turned out, her will had been revised shortly before her passing. All of her children, whether surviving or otherwise, were included with an equal portion. I suspect Aunt Joyce was involved in making this more equitable distribution. She was also the person who gave us one of Nanny's beautiful Persian rugs.

Anyway, I had still been doing my morning pages and following Julia Cameron's prompts from her book *The Artist's Way*. Several months previous, I had been pondering my dreams and wishes. If I had no limit of money, one of my dreams was to re-landscape our backyard. As it was, the large hill was held back with terraced railroad ties. Many of these had rotted. Others had been pushed and twisted from years of constant pressure and the freeze-thaw cycles of our climate. No matter what I planted, the yard looked disheveled and patched together. It didn't help that the underside of our porch cover was coming apart. In different, random places, the plaster had fallen off. This was my view from almost every window. Kent and I talked about what to do. Given the health challenges in our family at the time and the overwhelming task and expense of pulling out all those railroad ties and starting from scratch, we decided it would have to wait.

Even though I did not see how it could be possible, dreaming of having a beautiful backyard was therapeutic. I put my dream out into the "universe" and waited to see if the "universe" would respond. When word came that Nanny had left us some unexpected money, though not enough to complete the project as I had hoped, Kent offered his support. He wanted me to have my dream.

I received this gift with more than just gratitude. On difficult days when, despite the many assurances I was receiving, I still questioned whether or not things would turn out okay, I found great comfort in my yard. Here was an answered prayer from God. It was His gift, a token of His love, and an evidence of His awareness of my hopes and dreams. I also thanked Aunt Joyce and Nanny for helping it come to pass.

Perhaps it was the stress, but my health deteriorated. In addition to my emotional changes, I had a difficult time sleeping and often woke with terrible headaches. I was scheduled for surgery on December 10, 2004 to have the one tumor removed. If all went well, I'd be home in three days and mostly recovered by Christmas. This time, I would be sure to leave my staples in as long as possible. (As I have already mentioned, following the previous surgery, when they were taken out too soon, my incision separated.)

In the meantime, Janice had been nominated for royalty at the school dance. She was not yet sixteen. She was fifteen, and her birthday wasn't until the end of February. Janice knew of our wishes that she not date until she was sixteen. We did express our understanding that being nominated was an honor and agreed that she needed to go to the dance. It was a girl's choice event. We left the resolution of this dilemma in her hands. The dance was also scheduled for December 10.

In the end, Janice asked her father to go with her. I'm not sure if any girl has ever taken her father to a high school dance, but Janice did. She was a good sport for asking him, and he was a good sport for going. Luckily, Kent has a fun sense of humor and can be quite entertaining. When one of the girls in Janice's group did not have the money to pay for her and her date's meal, Kent took care of it. Because Janice's friends gathered frequently in our home, and Kent knew them all, many of them took a turn dancing with him as well. From the reports, everyone had a wonderful time.

Janice mentioned one girl at the dance ridiculed her for bringing her dad, but the next year, several girls asked if she would be taking her father again. If she was, they also wanted to take their dads. By that time, Janice was dating, and not interested in spending the evening with a parent.

A couple of days before my surgery, I recorded this scripture in my pages, "Behold, I say unto you that whoso believeth in Christ, doubting nothing, whatsoever he shall ask the Father in the name of Christ it shall be granted him; and this promise is unto all, even unto the ends of the earth" (Mormon 9:21.) In my pages, I told the Father I believed those words and asked if He would heal Janice. As I listened for a response, this is what I heard, "Be not afraid for I am with thee. Thy request shall be granted. My heart is drawn out towards thee in mercy and compassion. Keep my commandments. My hand is over all, even in your afflictions."

Kent gave me a priesthood blessing the night before I went in. He blessed me that all would be well and that I would have a quick recovery. (These promises would cause me some confusion later.) He also promised me I would return to my normal function without lasting problems. My strength and vigor would return. He also told me I would witness miracles.

That same night when I listened for the whisperings of the Spirit, I heard, "Thine afflictions shall be but a small moment. Be positive and uplifting."

I went in for surgery the next morning. That night, Kent went to the dance with Janice. While he was away, the nurse came in to check my postoperative vitals. I was still groggy from the anesthesia. When she checked the bandage over my incision, her eyes opened wide. "Your bandage is sopping wet."

"Is it blood?" I asked.

She shook her head. "No. I'm calling the doctor."

The neurosurgery resident came right in and checked the surgical dressing for himself then left to call my surgeon. A few minutes later, my neurosurgeon stood by the side of my bed. "Your incision is leaking spinal fluid. We're going to put in a few more stitches, and tomorrow we'll put in a lumbar drain."

Through all my years in nursing, I had not become aware of a lumbar drain. It's a good thing. Each one of us has what I refer to as a misery index. Whenever we go through something we use our misery index to determine how awful it is. When we stub our toe, we think, "Dang, my toe hurts, but not nearly as bad as when I rolled my ankle." With every discomfort or illness, we compare it to all the other miserable things we have listed on our personal misery index.

My misery index to that point in my life included a previous brain surgery, two partial nephrectomies, one with a bowel resection, three experiences with childbirth, one a stillbirth, breast infections, spinal cord surgery, pneumonia, and a really bad flu. That was all before my lumbar drain.

The next morning, the resident inserted the lumbar drain. If you've ever had a spinal tap or an epidural, it's the same thing. The only difference is that with the lumbar drain, they leave the tube in. Every hour, they drained more spinal fluid out. The hope was that in the absence of spinal fluid, the incision would heal.

I have never experienced such excruciating misery. I truly wondered how I could ever endure this agony for more than an hour, let alone three days. Your spinal fluid exerts pressure. When the fluid is removed, it creates a vacuum throughout your central nervous system. My head felt as though it was in a vice grip times ten. I could not open my eyes, I could not speak. Any movement or noise made me vomit violently and felt like torture. I could not feel my incision so I'm sure I was on a Morphine drip. I cannot imagine what the pain would have been like without it. With each hour, more fluid was drawn off. I felt myself becoming smaller and smaller, until I felt as though I were a single, tiny dot. "I'm disappearing," I told the nurse.

"Please help me," I pleaded with my Father in Heaven. My thoughts became a thread of, "Please, please, please." I came to the realization my idea of "all would be well, and I would have a quick recovery," was much different than the Lord's. I listened for His reply, but the only words that came back were, "But if not . . ."

I knew what they meant. In the book of Daniel is the story of Shadrach, Meshach, and Abed-nego. Since they wouldn't worship King Nebuchadnezzar's idols, he decided to kill them. The king stoked his furnaces seven times hotter than normal in preparation for casting them in. Before he did, the three believers bore their testimony to the king that they knew their God would deliver them, "BUT IF NOT," they would still trust in their Lord (see Daniel 3:18).

Many of God's most stalwart believers crossed my mind—John the Baptist, Abinadi, Joseph Smith, even the Savior Himself, Jesus Christ.

Did I still trust in Him? Even if He would not deliver me? I considered this, knowing He was my only hope. It was quite a different experience, there in the darkest hour I had ever known, to express my gratitude to my Father in Heaven and express my love to Him. My cries of, "Please, please, please," turned to, "But if not . . . I still love Thee, I still believe in Thee, I still trust in Thee."

My pain did not go away. I considered it a miracle I survived my three days of the lumbar drain. They took it out, and I still had to stay flat in bed. I had not been able to sit up since my surgery. When the nurse came in to help me up for the first time, the bed was wet. After having the drain in for three days, the hole would not seal. Spinal fluid continued to leak out. It took a suture and two more days before I could go home. I had been in the hospital for a week.

Ten days later when I went back to the doctor's to have my stitches taken out, I still could not sit up for more than an hour. Every time I tried, I felt that vacuum of fluid pulling on my brain. I couldn't eat and I couldn't sleep.

On the day Kent had to go back to work after the holidays, about five weeks later, I felt better. I could breathe, and I finally slept. I kept thinking, *I will pay for this tomorrow*. But that next morning, I felt better than I had the day before. As I read my scriptures, I came across this dramatic and powerful promise: "He [the Lord] giveth power to the faint; and to them that have no might he increaseth strength. . . . But they that wait upon the Lord shall renew their strength; they shall mount up with wings as eagles; they shall run, and not be weary; and they shall walk, and not faint" (Isaiah 40:29, 31).

The Spirit confirmed those words were mine. And from that day forward, my strength increased, and I eventually had a full recovery.

Sherri Dew, a faithful Mormon woman, made the comment that in every one of our lives comes that moment when we find out what we really believe. I believe I've had several of those moments throughout my life. Here's what I know:

Believing in God is a choice. We don't make that choice once, we make it every day. We make it in how we treat others and how we conduct ourselves in everything we do.

Secondly, God keeps His promises. He may not keep them the way we think He will, but in the end, He more than makes up any difference. He does visit us in our afflictions.

Thirdly, He does have all power. He could remove every trial, every challenge, and all suffering. But He honors choice, which also means He honors consequences. If our trial or suffering is of no benefit, I believe He will remove it if we ask. If, on the other hand, our challenge is part of completing our mission, He will not take away our destiny. I believe we agreed to this when we made the choice to be born.

We are all significant. Each one of us has a destiny. Every individual has great works to accomplish while in this life. Whether or not we acknowledge this and follow through on our mission is our choice.

I have spent a lot of time asking Him to help me understand why we must all die. How does He expect us to understand immortality and eternal life when we are mortal and not one of us will escape the finality of death? How can we understand His perfection and love when we live in this imperfect world He created?

I encourage you to ask Him these same questions. Don't accept anyone else's opinions and don't vent your frustrations to anyone but Him. Just as John the Baptist did, take your questions directly to Him.

I have received my answers. And I am reconciled. I could tell you what I know, but you might not believe me. If you hear it from Him directly, then you will believe. I testify that He lives. He hears. He answers.

30

HEALING

Although I experienced an eventual return of physical strength and stamina following my second brain surgery, I did notice some cognitive deficits with language. I think these were related more to the stress on my system from the lumbar drain than the surgery itself. The first of these changes was an inability to recognize familiar words. I could not immediately remember the meaning or the pronunciation. This lasted for several months and happened with random words at random times. The second thing I noticed was my diminished ability to understand what others said to me. I recognized they were speaking but could not connect meaning to their words. My poor family. They had to say everything twice. By the time they repeated a comment, my brain had finally processed what they were telling me. This went on for about a year.

Many times I wondered what had happened. Why did I start leaking spinal fluid after my brain surgery? What went wrong? For several years before Janice was born, when I worked as a patient relations representative for a hospital, I worked closely with Risk Management and was privy to many of the lawsuits brought against the hospital. I was very sensitive to the reality that a bad outcome does not necessarily indicate negligence on the part of the doctor or hospital. But I worried about my leaking fluid since it was more than likely I would need another brain surgery at some point in the future.

Several months later, I had to have additional surgery on three precancerous moles that had been shaved off in the doctor's office. A few days after the surgery, which took additional wedges of tissue around the moles, one of the three incisions opened up. All of them seemed to take a long time to heal.

Okay. It took me all of this to finally realize my body had an issue with healing. I recalled the incision from my first brain surgery had also opened. I thought it was from taking the staples out too early, but now I had to rethink that explanation. Kent was not surprised. He pointed to my diet as the culprit. I was probably the only person on the planet who could rationalize that a diet soda and a hostess cupcake constituted a well-balanced breakfast. Despite the fact that I exercised six days a week, I was not healthy. I made an appointment with a fitness and nutritional expert and began my journey toward helping my body to heal.

I came to a realization about the importance of nutrition. I also appreciated the necessity of resistance training. All my years of trudging in the basement on my Nordic track, stair stepper, and treadmill, had actually diminished my muscle mass. By eating nutritionally rich foods and following a resistance training program, my body improved its capacity to heal.

Isn't it a miracle the body has the ability to heal? A segment of the instructions in every cell has to do with repairing itself. I spent a great deal of time pondering the concept of healing and what more I could do to help my body. This led me to question how much influence I had over its processes. Did I have control over whether or not my tumors grew? Was there more I could do to stop them from growing?

There are a lot of interesting theories out there about healing. I think I've read almost all of them, though I may have missed a couple. My studies opened a new arena of questions for me personally. What is my relationship with my body? How is my spirit connected? What is the interface of my spirit and my physical being? I lay these questions down reverently at the feet of an Almighty Presence, knowing I am seeking to understand one of His mysteries.

What has been impressed upon me is that healing is a major theme of my life. (I believe it is a major theme in everyone's life.) With my body, every cut, scrape, puncture, burn, etc. has to heal. I had overlooked this incredible, natural, efficient mending. The damage could be the tiniest of insults, but if it didn't heal, it festered and eventually required intervention.

As I pondered this process, I came to an awareness of the importance of spiritual and emotional healing in my life as well. I believe my body is a metaphor of my spirit. How was my capacity to heal spiritually? Did every spiritual or emotional insult need attention? And how was this accomplished? How would I know if I had healed or if I was still wounded?

I was reminded of the dream I had when we lived in Arizona and I was praying about what we should do about having a family. In this dream, I was walking across a dark and desolate battlefield searching for a high-school friend. The casualties moaning in heaps all around me represented those who had been spiritually wounded.

I mentioned before that I've read a great deal about healing. Most of these texts focus on physical healing. Much of the information had to do with nutrition. I thought about what I was feeding my spirit. How was I spending my time and what information was I ingesting into my mind and heart?

As a trial, I cancelled our newspaper subscription. Wanting to be "informed," I generally spent about an hour every day reading through the paper. This was an interesting experiment. Since I am a member of the human race, I have always been interested in what is going on in the world. After about a month, I evaluated my life. What, if anything, had changed? How had this change affected me spiritually?

It is not my intention to malign the "media," but I noticed a huge change in the quality of my life. Given that most of what is reported is negative, the introduction of tragic, senseless, hopeless, and cruel events on a daily basis had a greater impact on my thoughts and emotions than I had realized. Now that we have digital access to almost anywhere in the world at any moment, we are bombarded with an abundance of calamity. For that month when I pushed the world's heartaches aside, my mood lightened, life became less stressful, and I felt more peace.

I learned that by reading the paper and involving myself in stranger's stories, I was expending vital mental and emotional energy. Without this daily vicarious investment, my heart pursued more meaningful relationships with people near and dear to me. Life became richer and more significant.

Recognizing the dramatic and desirable changes this brought, for a time I also removed TV and radio. I refer to that time as my "spiritual fast." I filled my heart and mind with things that inspired, encouraged hope, and increased my capacity to love.

The scriptures and good books became my food, and I feasted. I found tremendous power in this scripture as the Savior spoke to a wounded people, "Will ye not now return unto me, and repent of your sins, and be converted, that I may heal you?" (3 Nephi 9:13).

I recognized that I carried many worries rooted in memories of illness and loss. This was the only life I had, how could I move past the sorrow? I understood the Savior's power and ability to heal, but I was desperate to know what that might feel like for me personally.

Janice had another MRI to check the status of her tumors. Her appointment was on a Monday. The Sunday before was a fast Sunday. In my pages during the sacrament at church I wrote, "I do believe the promises thou hast made. I partake of this sacrament – this emblem of thy sacrifice for me – with gratitude. I am grateful for the law of the fast, for this opportunity to reach out to thee and to be obedient to thy commandments. I love thee.

I am grateful for the assurances and peace I have felt regarding Janice's appointment tomorrow."

As I listened, these were the words I received in my heart, "Be of good cheer, for, lo, I am with thee and will stand by thee in all of thy trials. I shall be in thy front, thy back, and shall bear thee up on either side. Thou shalt witness my hand. Thou shalt feel of my love and my power. I desire to bless thee, for thou hast been grateful and acknowledged my hand. The riches of the world are mine to give to whomsoever I will. Go forward in faith and gratitude and thou shalt have great joy."

How sweet it was the next day when Janice's MRI revealed no changes. Everything was stable. She also had an eye exam, which confirmed her vision had improved. The tumor on her optic nerve was no longer leaking fluid.

I saw this as a gift. I knew this did not mean Janice was in the clear forever, but on that day, and at that time, receiving that good news was sweet. It felt delicious. The relief filled my heart and in that moment, I experienced great joy.

In the beginning as I practiced listening to the impressions I received, I was afraid to hear what the Lord might have to say to me. I worried He might get frustrated with my lack of faith or my persistent inadequacies. I imagined Him ranting, "How many times do I have to tell you?" or "What is your problem, why can't you believe me?"

The more I listen, the more I love Him. He is patient, long-suffering, and so kind. His words heal my heart. They heal my soul and give me courage to move forward. They speak of peace and trust and a magnificent life unfolding before me. And consistently since that day before Janice's appointment, they always begin with the same words, "Be of good cheer, for, lo, I am with thee."

He has given me permission to be happy.

31

ANITA WARNED ME

I haven't written much about my brother, Rob, and his journey with VHL. In almost every way, his journey has been far more dramatic than my own. I haven't included much about Rob because I am sensitive about trying to tell his story. So much is lost when an experience is narrated by an onlooker rather than the one moving the scenery. Not only that, but events change us. They reshape our view of the world, recalibrate our misery index, and give us new understanding and insight. I could talk about what Rob has been through and the many challenges he has faced, but I cannot convey his inner landscape where his experiences have refined and molded his character.

This chapter, therefore, is not an attempt to tell Rob's story. On many occasions, however, our lives intersected. Throughout my life, Rob and I were close even though four years and a sister separated us. We shared many of the same interests, had many of the same personality traits, and Rob and I looked more alike than any others in the family. We looked like our mom, where Sue took after our dad. As we grew older, married, had kids, and went through surgeries for VHL, we commiserated. Much of this was done over the phone since Rob and his family lived in Michigan where Rob worked for Chrysler.

Rob's wife, Anita, has become another sister to me. She lost her biological father when she was two, and her mother remarried while Anita was still young. Anita was no stranger to trials. She loved being a devoted mother and wife. One of the greatest joys of being a mother is seeing your children succeed. Rob and Anita have five wonderful children. They are bright, athletic, talented, and attractive. I told Anita I wanted to share in the joy of her children's successes. I wanted to know of all the awards, championships, and perfect report cards. I wanted to celebrate their victories. And there have been many. Anita has cheered for my children as well. Through the years, though I have not mentioned much of our relationship, Rob and Anita have been a great source of strength. And through Rob's own trials, he has shown tremendous faith.

In October of 2007, Anita warned me, "Rob looks a lot like your mother." She mentioned his speech and how he talked like Mom used to as well. Was there something different about the way Mom talked? I couldn't remember her having problems with her speech.

I'm glad Anita warned me.

Anita's brother, Charlie, and I arrived on the same flight in the Detroit airport. He had a business meeting in Ohio after his visit with Anita. Because of this, he had a rental car and would drive us to Anita's instead of having someone come and pick us up. After a quick dinner, we drove straight to the RIM, the Rehabilitation Institute of Michigan, where Rob was a patient.

Rob had undergone yet another surgery two weeks earlier. I couldn't count them all, he'd had so many. Was this his sixth or seventh brain surgery? I wasn't sure how to even count this one since it included a surgery on his cervical spine as well.

Three years previous, it was discovered that Rob had a large tumor on his brain stem. He was told that only one surgeon in the country could remove it, a doctor in Phoenix at the Barrow

Neurological Institute. He told Rob there was a 40 percent chance he might not make it through the surgery. This would already be his fifth brain surgery. What a miracle when Rob survived and his only deficit was one paralyzed vocal cord. Even that healed with speech therapy and time.

Fast forward two years from that surgery. Rob didn't feel well. He was losing the use of his right leg and fell at work. Both feet were going numb. A scan showed an ugly tumor in the front of his spinal cord. No doctor wanted to touch it, knowing it would be difficult to reach with a questionable outcome. After four months of losing function, Rob finally found a surgeon who was willing to do the surgery. But there was no miracle this time. After the surgery, which involved removing six tumors, Rob lost the use of his right leg and the functional use of his left. After four weeks in Rehab, Rob learned how to control his left leg enough to walk short distances and to manage stairs. He learned to drive himself to work with a left foot pedal, pull his wheelchair out of the backseat, and wheel himself into his office. Though he moved slowly and with great effort, he was independent and could take care of his own needs.

About this time, I discovered a growing tumor in my own spinal cord. Rob encouraged me to get it removed sooner than later. I followed his advice and had the surgery in June of 2007. Although the neurosurgeon monitored the function of my nerves throughout the surgery and no problems were noted, I came out of the surgery numb from my waist down. Fortunately, I was fully functional and though I still remain slightly numb to this day, much of my sensation has returned.

About three months after my surgery, when the doctor told Rob he had another brain tumor that needed to be removed, Anita told me the two of them wept. But when the surgeon also told them there was one in his cervical spine that needed to come out, they left the office in shock and despair. Knowing the risks, Rob debated whether or not to have the surgery. The doctor could not promise Rob that he would have the use of his arms or if he would be able to breathe on his own. If Rob chose not to have the surgery, it would only be a matter of time before he lost the function anyway.

After much prayer and fasting, Rob decided to go ahead with the surgery. I waited anxiously for Anita's call, letting me know how the surgery went. At first the news was good. Rob could breathe on his own, and he was moving his arms. Later, she would call to let me know he could move his arms, but he had lost the proprioception, the nerves that let the brain know their position. In essence, he could move his arms and hands, but unless he could see where his hands and arms were, the movement was not functional.

On every level, my heart leaned in their direction. I knew what this arm movement looked like. Before Mom became a quadriplegic and lost the complete use of her arms, she lacked coordination and every movement was awkward and uncontrolled. I already knew how it felt to have someone I loved in that condition. I prayed for Anita, knowing how difficult it would be for her to watch Rob struggle with simple arm and hand movements.

My pages did bring me comfort. On September 18 he had the surgery. On the 19th I heard these words in my heart, "I am with Rob. He is in my hands. Trust me. Believe in me. Be still and know that I am God. He is securing a place for him and his family in the Kingdom of God. What greater work can he do? Be not discouraged, nor dismayed. I do not delight in his suffering, but I do have desires to bless him."

As Rob was moved to the rehab facility on the 24th, I heard, "I am with Rob and will bless him. He is in my power. He shall be comforted. Anita shall receive strength beyond her own capacity. His life shall be full and he shall have joy. For after much tribulation, cometh the blessings. Take courage, give them hope and encouragement."

The next day, I made arrangements to go to Michigan and offer my help and support.

I'm embarrassed to admit this was the first time I had visited Rob and Anita since they moved to Michigan seventeen years before. But I had to go. Rob and I have shared sacred thoughts and feelings for many years. We had received our patriarchal blessings, in which we had both been warned of trials, on the same day. I hoped I could give Rob comfort, understanding, and support.

I'm glad Anita warned me. When I saw Rob, he looked so small. He had lost over forty pounds, dropping from 180 to about 140 pounds. He moved his arms to wave, but they wobbled with little coordination. And when he tried to eat, it took such concentration for him to stab a piece of food with his modified fork and then bring it safely to his mouth. When he talked, I understood what Anita meant. He had to speak slowly, or his words slurred. The cadence of his speech reminded me of Mom's.

During my week-long stay, Rob and I visited at length. He wanted to talk about Mom, mostly. He had moved to Michigan during the last years of her life, right after she had become quadriplegic. He wanted to know everything. What could she move, and did she ever have any therapy? I sensed in both Rob and Anita a longing to touch Mom again. They had a new awareness of her struggle as if they had just discovered her handicap for the first time. Her life was now their experience. And they wished they had been more in tune with her needs.

I could see Mom in Rob in other ways as well—the way he was patient with himself when simple things, such as rolling over, took such incredible effort. The way he accepted his situation without anger or bitterness. And his tenacious determination to master skills that were once unconscious movements. And every day I saw improvement.

When I had taken care of my mom, I felt every day as if I were taking care of myself. I did not feel that way with Rob. Sometimes I would stop, breathe in, and take a gut-check. Was this my future as well? Was I once again seeing myself? There was nothing in my mind or heart to ever confirm or dismiss these questions. I was reminded, however, how our memories color our lives. We see everything through the lens of our experience. I viewed Rob through the lens of what I had been through with our mother. I am amazed how everything we go through gives us new insight into what happened in the past.

Spending time with Rob also reoriented my priorities. The numbness in my own legs was no longer a problem. Every day I went down with him to therapy where he painstakingly stacked, then un-stacked, a bunch of cups, working on his manual dexterity. I was reminded he was securing a place for him and his family in the Kingdom of God. And it didn't have anything to do with the cups. "My people must be tried in all things, that they may be prepared to receive the glory that I have for them, . . .and he that will not bear chastisement is not worthy of my kingdom" (Doctrine and Covenants 136:31).

There is something inspiring about witnessing the triumph of the human spirit. We can worship fame and fortune and all the superficial luxuries and celebrities of this life, but when we behold the strength and goodness of the human will in overcoming difficult obstacles, we have seen true greatness. We know it when we see it because we feel it. I felt it that week with Rob. In every day and hour, he was a great man. Being with him gave me a new resolve to try harder and be better. I learned it isn't important what we are asked to endure. It is how we endure it. Rob taught me that. He showed me the way, just as Mom had showed him.

32

MY ENDING OF THE DREAM

Our women's writing group has been going for several years now. We meet twice a month and I wouldn't miss one of our gatherings. These women have become part of my story. We read, we talk, we laugh, but mostly we share. In the beginning, it was casual. When I brought something I'd written it was usually a story about my old crushes or memories of my summers at Nanny's cabin in Island Park, Idaho. They were easy and light. But each week as we bonded closer, my stories became more difficult. "I'm sorry," I'd tell the group, "it's therapy again."

They never seemed to mind. They cried and rejoiced with me through all of my triumphs and tragedies. At one point, I decided I was ready. It was time to tell my story. I trusted these women with my life.

Memories did not turn out exactly as I remembered them. For example, I did not realize I had such major relationship issues with my mother until they announced themselves boldly on the page. I should have known. Several years after Mom died, but before I began this memoir, I had a dream. I walked into the bedroom where Mom stayed when she was with us, and I was surprised to see her lying there, as even in the dream I knew she had passed on several years before.

"Mom, how long have you been here?" I felt terrible, thinking she had been there all that time without any attention.

Her eyes narrowed and her lips quivered. "You've just left me here."

I awoke in a sweat, grateful it was only a dream and that Mom was not still in what was now my son's bedroom.

Although the focus of this memoir has been the role God has played in my life and what my experiences have taught me about Him, I have discovered even greater insight as I have recorded these events. I now see this is the story of my relationship with God and how it has changed and changed me through the phases and challenges of my life. Consider this my explanation for who I am and why I came to be that way.

This memoir does not include much about the regular days, the ones where I spent hours in my yard or did the laundry or rode out to the mules with Kent. There is another, normal part of me that is not in these pages.

Stephanie is the one who keeps saying, "You have to get this published."

I keep asking, "Who would want to take this journey with me? Who would want to read about all of this?" If, by chance, you have taken this long and difficult walk through my footsteps, I hope it hasn't been too heavy. I hope there's been something meaningful to make the effort worth your while.

There's more I could write. I wanted to talk about my son, Andrew, who is getting ready to leave on his mission for the Church. He is nineteen and so excited to serve. He'll be one of those young men in suits and ties you see in your neighborhood, walking or riding a bike. Yes, sigh, one of those kids you hate to see on your doorstep. But he's my son, and he's a good kid. The best part is, before he left, though he didn't seem bothered, I needed to know if he had VHL. We met with the geneticist and they took Andrew's blood. We waited six weeks, but the genetic test came back negative. He does not have VHL. This is one of the greatest joys of my life. I wanted you to know about that.

I also wanted you to know Janice is in love. I'm not sure how it's going to turn out. Janice didn't get to choose this disease, and if given a choice, I doubt if she would say, "Yes, I think I want VHL." How then does she ask anyone else to willingly take VHL on as a part of their life? But that's exactly what she is asking of someone who wants to marry her. How does this young man then explain to his family and friends that although he is healthy with every hope of a bright future, he is choosing to live with the ramifications of having VHL? And if his loved ones should object or discourage him, Janice can give no argument in defense. How does Janice ask this sacrifice from anyone, especially from someone she loves? I did not know I had VHL when I dated and made the decision to be married. If I had known beforehand, I'm not sure I could have answered these questions either.

In addition to the things I wanted to tell you, there are other things I wanted to send home with you in a nice little package, but I couldn't find a way to wrap them up. I can't tell you how my life will end. I mentioned earlier the occasion where my mother told me, "If I can go through this so you don't have to, I am happy to do it."

I told my brother, Rob, about that, and I could never convince him that he would not have to go through what Mom did—that she had already done it for us. He never felt that offering on her part was for him.

Rob had that horrible surgery in September of 2007 where he lost the use of his arms and the ability to walk again. This was when I visited with him in Michigan. Rob made it his goal to return to work and provide for his family. By June, though he had not fully recovered, he made it back to work with the use of a wheelchair. Anita told me he would wake up several hours early every morning in order to give himself time to shower, dress, and shave. He did this all from his chair, with limited use of his hands. Anita would drive him to work and pick him up again. How he managed is the miracle of it all. He told Anita how one day he was trying to make it up a small hill at work. His hands were not strong enough to roll the chair up the slope, until someone pushed him from behind. When he got to the top, feeling so grateful for the help, he turned to say, "Thank you," but no one was there.

Rob never complained. He had an appointment to learn how to drive a special van. He didn't want to be a burden to Anita and the kids for rides to and from work. As the day for his first driving lesson drew near, Rob realized he was losing his vision. Anita called to let me know they had cancelled his appointment. I knew she was scared. What could possibly be causing the loss of his vision?

In my silent prayers, I heard the words, "Rob's time is short. Help prepare Anita." These were not the words I wanted to hear.

It was several weeks before an eye appointment indicated the problem was not with his eyes. It was a few more weeks before an MRI could be scheduled. A week or so after that, Anita called on the telephone. With emotion breaking in her voice she told me the MRI showed more than ten brain tumors, some with large cysts. His spinal cord had erupted with numerous tumors as well. They seemed to be everywhere and were growing out of control. Rob had grown more tumors in that last year than he had grown in his entire life. Their neurosurgeon told them there was nothing he could do. Fortunately, the NIH was willing to see him. In December of 2008, I met Rob and Anita in the Baltimore airport and traveled with them to the hotel.

Rob had improved since I'd seen him at the rehab facility in Detroit. He greeted me with my usual nickname, "Bino!" Although he sat in the wheelchair listing to one side or the other similar to the way Mom had, and shrugged his shoulders as Mom once did, he did not remind me of Mom. The affection in his eyes and voice set him apart.

Anita is such a tiny thing. At 5'4" and about 100 pounds, I have no idea how she maneuvered Rob down that narrow aisle and into his seat on the airplane, along with managing his wheelchair and all of their luggage. That's why I wanted to meet them in the airport so I could at least be there to help Rob and Anita get to the hotel.

The next day, they met with the neurosurgeons at the NIH, and found Rob did have one tumor in his cervical spine they wanted to remove. This surgery would at least preserve what little arm function he had left. They could do nothing about his declining vision.

We all returned home, but the week before Christmas of 2008, on Anita's birthday, Rob and Anita returned to the NIH where Rob had another surgery. Although he was weak, he came through the surgery without anymore deficits. We celebrated this, but given his loss of vision and weakened body, Rob was no longer able to return to work. Add to this stress, the floundering American economy and the impending implosion of the auto industry, including Chrysler where Rob had worked.

When Rob's son opened his mission call in March of 2009, and learned he had been called by the prophet to serve in the Dominican Republic, I was there. Rob's son was here in Utah, attending college at BYU, but we shared the event with Rob, Anita, and the rest of the family in Michigan on a webcam. Rob looked good. He was sitting up in his wheelchair, talking, and smiling. I wanted to capture that day, wondering how long his health might last.

What is the Lord's definition of "short"? And how was I supposed to help prepare Anita?

By the first of April, Rob was showing signs of declining. He was sleeping more, didn't have as much energy, and speaking was becoming more difficult.

I experienced another serendipitous event. Our writing group had been attending some workshops at the local library on doing personal histories. The most recent one in March had presented a segment on preparing ethical wills. I had never heard of an ethical will before, but in essence, it passes on what life has meant to you, your hopes and dreams for the future, and those traits and characteristics you would like to pass on to your posterity. I approached Anita about whether or not she thought Rob would want to leave an ethical will. I told Anita I would be willing to help Rob write his. With Rob's consent, on several occasions over the phone, Rob told me the things he wanted to include. He shared tender feelings about the love he had for this world and for his wife and children. He spoke of his gratitude for his body and for all those who had done so much to help him and his family. He spoke of his dreams for his children, and described the kind of people he hoped they would become. Most of all, he wanted to thank Anita and let her know how deeply he loved her. "I would go to hell and back for you, since you have already done so for me."

At the end of April 2009, it was my privilege to spend a week with Rob while he was in the hospital. Because of the large tumors on Rob's brainstem, he'd lost the ability to swallow. Anita and Rob didn't realize this, and he had been aspirating food and fluid into his lungs, instead of it going down into his stomach. As a result, he had developed a healthy pneumonia, which landed him in the hospital.

Before my departure, a friend recommended I read the book, *Final Gifts*, written by two hospice nurses. In the book, they explain that as patients draw near to death, they have specific experiences the authors describe as "near death awareness." Descriptions by patients of the things they felt and saw were similar to what I had heard patients report while I was working as a nurse in oncology.

In Michigan, I took a taxi to the hospital. I opened Rob's hospital room door to see Anita there with Rob, sitting on his bed, talking with him. Rob stared into her eyes, nodding, a smile on his face. He absolutely adored her.

"Bino!" He called out to me when I walked in.

He had lost even more weight than the last time I had seen him, but thanks to his good care, he was clean, shaven, and comfortable. As we talked, I could see and hear how difficult speech was becoming. He spoke slowly so his words were distinct and articulate. I slept on a small sofa in his room at night so Anita could go home, take care of the house and kids, and get some needed rest.

Those nights are sacred to me now. Rob no longer had the strength to turn himself, and I was happy to move him at his request.

His nights were restless. One of my first nights, Rob called me out of my sleep, "Come on, Bino, we've got to move."

"Would you like me to turn you?" I asked, peeling back my blanket and adjusting my sweat pants before I stood.

Rob shook his head, looking wide eyed around the room, "There are people in this room."

Because of the book, *Final Gifts*, and my own nursing experiences, I knew Rob was straddling two worlds. I had no doubt that, although I could not see them, there were in fact people in that room. Rob was lucid and oriented. If I had asked him the time of night, the last time he had been turned, or the minute of his last medication, he would have responded exactly.

Speaking of the people in the room I could not see, I asked Rob, "Do they want you to go with them?"

He shook his head, "No, they just want to be acknowledged."

"Do they need us to do anything?" I asked.

Rob shook his head again, "No, they just need to know we're here. 'We're here,'" he told them.

I watched Rob's eyes as he followed movement I could not see. I studied his expressions that changed from amazement, to wonder, and back to amazement again. After a few minutes he looked back at me, "Do you think they are here to help me?"

I nodded. "Yes. I believe they are here to help, and to give you comfort."

Rob and I shared other amazing experiences with each other during those nights. On one occasion, he couldn't sleep, and we spoke about the reality that his remaining time was short.

There were things he needed to say to his family. They needed to know he was okay with going. "I don't want to go, Bino, but I don't want to be a burden."

I understood. After all I had been through with Mom, I didn't want my family to go through it either. "Will you promise me, Rob, that when it's my turn, you will come for me? I don't want to be a burden either. Will you please come for me?"

"I promise, Bino, I will."

When I left Michigan at the end of the week, I knew it was the last time I would see Rob until he came for me as promised. In my heart, I heard the words, "I am with Rob. I shall receive him with open arms and say to him, 'Well done thou good and faithful servant. Enter now into my rest.' Support Anita. Love her and assure her she has been a celestial companion. She has been a wonderful source of strength. I will bless her in every way."

Rob died on May 28, 2009. He and his family had the opportunity to share many sacred experiences together. Anita told me the other day she witnessed many miracles during the time of Rob's struggles. For my Christmas present this year, she is going to write them down and send me a copy.

When I was young, I loved the wind. We lived on Vista View Drive at the base of the Wasatch Mountains, overlooking the opening to the Emigration Canyon. Every morning, the rising heat of the valley air pushed a breeze up the canyon, which flowed back down in the evening as the air cooled. Whenever I noticed the trees swaying from my window, I would run outside and feel the wind. I loved to stand at just the right angle so the wind pushed my face and lifted the hair from my forehead. I listened for its whispers through the leaves and gauged its power by seeing how far I could lean in. I opened my mouth and tasted its breath, whether it was hot or cold on my lips. And I tipped my head back so I could smell where it had been. Did it stink of stagnant brine as it lifted off the Great Salt Lake to the west, or did it carry the scent of rattlesnakes and scrub oak from the mountains to the east? I often marveled, as I opened my eyes, that although I could taste it, feel it, hear it, and smell it, I could not see the wind. I could only experience its power and witness its influence on me and everything it touched.

I suppose the same is true of God. I have not seen Him with my eyes open either.

I don't know how my story will end or what trials I may yet face. I don't know if my mother's wish to "go through all of this so I don't have to," will apply to me or not. With that in mind, I can't end with that dream of my mother lying in bed angry, saying, "You've just left me here."

I feel compelled to end the dream. I see myself standing at the side of her bed, assuring her, "I don't have the power to move you from this place, but you were right, there is someone better."

I know Him, for I have felt Him. He has burned with power in my heart, encircled me in the arms of His love, and offered peace to my soul. He whispers joy into my days, gives me courage, and changes my heart. He is the source of all my strength, my faith, my hope, and my love. He is the light and life of this world. He is the light and life within me.

I want to be there on that day and see with my own eyes when, in His power and glory, the Savior Jesus Christ, the Redeemer of all mankind, takes my mother by the hand and reforms her crippled body into its resurrected perfection. I want to watch as Mom stands and stares in wonder at her perfect hands, now capable of touch and feeling. I want to be a witness as the Savior wipes away all the tears she never shed, relieves all the pain she never admitted, heals all the suffering she never acknowledged, and releases all the love she never expressed.

In the end of my dream, that is the moment when I take my mother in my arms. We embrace as mother and daughter, sharing a deep appreciation for what the other has endured.

A NOTE ABOUT VHL

Although VHL is generally an inherited mutation, it is estimated that 20% of all people with VHL are new mutations and have no family history. The children of these individuals, however, are at risk of inheriting the gene from their affected parent. If you would like more information about this disease, please go to www.vhl.org

Although I am a Mormon with VHL, the vast majority of people with VHL are not Mormons, and very few Mormons have VHL. VHL is a rare genetic disorder that occurs in populations worldwide.

22716758R00120

Made in the USA
Charleston, SC
01 October 2013